Built TO OUTLAST the STORM

The 12 Points of Turning a Setback into a Major Comeback

JAMILA T. DAVIS

Copyright © 2020 by Jamila T. Davis   All rights reserved.

This book or any portion thereof may not be reproduced or used in any manner whatsoever without the express written permission of the publisher, except for the use of brief quotation in a book review.

This book is a nondenominational, faith-based instruction manual. It was created to inspire, motivate and uplift readers to overcome obstacles. The author shares the strategies she has utilized, both spiritual and practical, to push past adversity. This book in not written to promote any set of religious beliefs, although it does encourage readers to be open to receiving assistance from their "Higher Power," as they know Him. The author does not claim to have originated any techniques or principles shared in this book. She has simply formulated a system of proven strategies, from her research and life experience.

Printed in the United States of America.

First Printing, 2020

LCCN: 2020910258
ISBN: 9780997675429

Voices International Publications
196-03-Linden Blvd. St. Albans, NY 11412
"Changing Lives One Page at a Time."
www.vocseries.com www.voicesbooks.com

Foreword

It all seemed to happen in the blink of an eye. Suddenly I was back in a similar space I was in a little less than three years ago, when I was still incarcerated. I came home on a mission! I was determined to gain back everything I lost and more. It was that inner drive in me that enabled me to build up a 100,000 + social media following, be featured in several television series, including CBS's *Pink Collar Crimes and* BET's *American Gangster: Trap Queens Series.* Just as I envisioned it on the bunk bed of my prison cell, I had made it to become an international motivational speaker and influencer who inspired hundreds of thousands of people to overcome adversity and become their greatest self.

My life had literally become the manuals that I had written while incarcerated, and just when I thought I had it all figured out, the Covid 19 Pandemic hit hard. Instantly, life seem to come to a sqreaching halt! Speaking engagements were canceled and hundreds of thousands of dollars of contracts were on hold.

My first instinct was to panic. I feared going backward after I had worked so hard to gain back everything I lost. You see, I came home from prison with very little, except my family's support. I was accustomed to a luxury lifestyle that I didn't have the privilege to sustain. What I had was drive and ambition like it was nobody's business. I was determined to walk in my purpose and make everyday living in the free-world count, and that I did!

At first, I didn't take the Pandemic seriously. I thought I could wait it out and it all would be over. However, as the days turned into weeks, and the weeks turned into months, I realized I would have to settle in, just like I did in prison. Adopting the principles I learned through my prior journey, I realized I had to make the best out of my time. This book you are reading was written a little over nine years ago.

With a release date long overdue, I decided to use my time during the epidemic to edit and finally release this book. As I read the chapters each day, the words strengthened me. I quickly realized the content in this book was extremely relatable to this current time. As I began to apply the principles, it positioned me to not just survive during this current state but thrive. I realized what I perceived to be a setback was a setup for a major comeback. It all started with my perception.

We have the power to channel any circumstance and make it work together for our good. I decided to take back my power. In doing so, this system revealed in this book was proven yet again to work.

For anybody who is feeling down or thinking you are defeated, this is the road map for you. You can overcome any adversity and land back on top! There is a reason you are still alive. You were built to outlast the storm!

Table of Contents

Foreword. 3
Table of Contents 5
Introduction 11
I. Changing Your Perspective. 17
II. Partnership with Your "Higher Power" 35
III. Taking Time Out to Meditate 51
IV. Learning from the Past, then Letting it Go. 65
V. Figuring Out What You Can Do 81
VI. Learning to Care for "Self". 97
VII. Tapping into Your Purpose 113
VIII. Giving Back. 129
IX. The Virtue of Persistence and Determination 145
X. Solution Focused! 157
XI. Enjoying the Journey of Life 169
XII. Perfect Practice 183
    Point 1: "What I perceive is what I'll receive,
        so I must take control over what I believe!" *184*

Point 2: "When the storm comes, I need a safety tower;
so I reach out to my "Higher Power." 184

Point 3: "I can change my course, it's never too late!
But first I must stop and meditate." 184

Point 4: "If I hold on to shame and guilt, my spirit will always be low.
So, I will learn from my past, acknowledge my mistakes, and
then simply let them go!". 184

Point 5: "When life seems hopeless, I must change my point of view.
That's how I regroup and figure out what I can do!" . . .184

Point 6: "I am my greatest asset, the temple that holds my wealth.
So, I must make me a priority and always care for "self." .184

Point 7: "Life without a mission is empty, dull, and worthless!
In order to find fulfillment, I must discover my purpose." .184

Point 8: "If I choose to be selfish, I'll always suffer from lack. To open
the doors of abundance, I must learn how to give back.". .184

Point 9: "Despite my opposition and what others say or believe,
I've got a made-up mind, no turning back.
I'm determined to succeed!". 185

Point 10: "My focus is my focus and my focus doesn't change.
It's nothing you can do to make my focus rearrange!" . . .185

Point 11: "If I purposely rid myself of all anger, worry, and strife, I'll
learn to embrace each day, enjoying this journey of life!" .185

Point 12: "Now that I have a plan, I know I won't fail! I'll practice
every point, until I have them nailed!" 185

On top of every other adversity, we have had to face, now Covid 19. If you are anything like me, you may have had big plans that you had all mapped out. Now you feel helpless and defeated because you realize you are not really in control. Obstacles happen to reshape our thinking and force us to grow. Will you choose to use this time to discover the equal reward that lies within this current life event? Trust me, it's there, and these points will help you find it!

First, change will not come until you embrace Point #1, changing your perspective. It is going to be what you choose to see. This is what you will ultimately get. Then there is Point #2, reaching out to your Higher Power. When you know you no longer have the control you thought you had, that is when it is time to seek God for help. The rest of the points focus on shifting our mindset and positioning our spirits to endure what's up ahead. You will see as you practice each point, you will begin to nail each lesson of life and make perseverance a lifestyle!

July 16, 2008

It was a bright sunny day—a day I'll never forget. I woke up with butterflies in my stomach. Immediately, I rolled over and took out my bible. Reciting the Twenty-third Psalm, I built up the faith to get out the bed and brush my teeth. I had been waiting for over five years to finally deal with this federal case that was lingering over my head, and today was finally my sentencing day. I prayed tirelessly for years. I had every preacher, prophet and evangelist I could find praying, too. They told me I was coming out of the courtroom like pure gold. I was nervous and, at the same time, anxious. After being on house arrest for close to two years, awaiting my sentence, I desperately wanted to be free!

It all started on April 3, 2003. I remember that day, too, oh, so well. An FBI Fraud Alert was issued against me. It was the beginning of the end of my empire crumbling. I was a twenty-five-year-old, successful multi-millionaire. As a financial service company owner and a real estate investor, I had cornered the real estate market in Alpine, New Jersey. Controlling over 30 million dollars in large, high-end estates sold to rappers, entertainers, sports players and other celebrities, I was at the height of my game. I had it all, money, power, status and success. Yet, in the blink of an eye, a high-profiled FBI investigation compromised everything I worked so hard to gain.

Before I walked out the door, I hugged and kissed my children. My son was eleven and my daughter was nine years old. I held them tightly and assured them both I'd be home for dinner. With my gospel music blasting, I prepared my mind and soul for my fate. Pulling up to the Federal Courthouse in Newark, New Jersey in my brand new, Cadillac Escalade, I went to court alone. I didn't want to take my family through the potential trauma that was up ahead. Using my large, black Chanel, sunglasses to cover my face, I hopped out the truck with fake confidence. Holding my head high, I entered the courtroom. To my surprise, it was filled with reporters. I quickly located my lawyer and stood by his side. The end was near and I felt it! My heart begin to pound rapidly as sweat poured down my face.

"Your Honor, I apologize to the court and my family for everything I've done and the pain that I've caused so many others. I'm truly remorseful for all my poor choices. Please sir, I beg you to find it in your heart to give me another chance. I promise you I won't let you down. Please give me another opportunity to be a better mother to my kids. I promise if you grant me that one wish, I will never, ever commit a crime again. I promise," I sobbed loudly. After pouring my heart out to the judge and begging for his mercy, it was time to be sentenced. The words I heard next would repeat in my mind for years to come. "You are hereby sentenced to serve one hundred and fifty-one months in federal prison," Judge Jose Linares said as he banged his gavel.

Immediately, my body went numb. It took me a minute to calculate the months into years. "Twelve-and a half years! No, no, no I can't do this!" I screamed in my head. Before I could gather my thoughts, the judge revoked my bail, and the sheriffs escorted me to a tiny cell in the back of the chambers.

Tears flowed uncontrollably down my face. In my mind, there was no way I could handle what was next. My heart began to race. I felt like I was watching my own funeral. All I could think about were my poor children. This morning would be the last morning they would see me in the free world for the next decade. Trying to digest the reality of what just occurred, I took a deep breath and closed my eyes. "Dear God, please take my life. I can't endure what's next. This is too painful to bear!"

Introduction

Life is an obstacle course, which consists of a series of tests and trials. Trials are sent to challenge us to grow and to help guide us to fulfill our purpose on earth. They are simply unavoidable! Inevitably, we will all have to face some trying times in life. The only way to get through our trials, is to actually go through them; there is no such thing as shortcuts!

Many of us spend a great deal of time, trying to circumvent problems, by looking for a quick fix or an easy way out. Our crafty maneuvers often delay our advancement, keeping us stuck longer in undesirable situations. The only way to master life is to embrace our trials. Instead of fearing obstacles, we must courageously stand up to them. We learn to do this by focusing on the reward, or what good will come out of every fiery situation we face. When we overcome our fears and change our perspective, life becomes easier. Instead of feeling like a victim, we have the power to take charge and become the victor!

It is important to understand that nothing happens in life by chance. We were all placed on this earth with an assignment and a purpose in mind. Obstacles lead us into God's plan for our lives. When fiery trials spark, they force us to see what's really important and what's not. Many of us get lost in the hustle and bustle of life. We become so preoccupied with people, places, and things that we often neglect what matters the most—our relationship with God. In this case, trials are sent to give us a reality check. They are the warning signals that alert us we are headed on the wrong path.

Knowing most obstacles we face have a purpose, or an opportunity for reward, it is up to us to explore the meaning behind them. When we discover this important element, the pain becomes bearable. Understanding the "why," soothes our irritation and empowers us with the strength we need to push through the process.

Life is all about advancement and growth. As we pass each test, we are promoted to the next level. Yet, each level of advancement comes with new challenges and hurdles we must overcome. In order to be promoted, we must pass the test. If not, we will stay bound and continue to experience the same test in different forms. It is important to understand the test will not go away until we pass it! Many of us try to ditch our tests by running.

For example, we may experience a rough time in our relationships, so we separate from people, only to get involved in a new relationship and have to experience the same sort of issues. Instead of facing the reality of our problems, we often take the easy way out and blame others for our own misfortunes. When we don't face the reality of our dilemma, it disables us.

Consequently, we become entrapped in an unhappy cycle of constant tribulations, all because we did not pass the test. The good news is, we do not have to remain stuck. Now, it's time to equip ourselves to overcome!

This book was created sincerely with you in mind. It is a road map of how to turn any adversity, or setback, into a major comeback. Life was not intended to be unpleasant. We can learn to enjoy life, no matter what situations we encounter! Joy comes from within. When we learn to master "self," we become the creators of our own happiness. This book will challenge you to look within. You will learn how to take the necessary steps to become victorious in every situation you encounter.

The road map enclosed in this book was developed by my sweat, pain, and tears. Starting at an early age, I experienced many triumphs and defeats. In a hot pursuit for money, prestige, and power, I soared to the top of my field, becoming a self-made, multi-millionaire by the age of twenty-five. I felt as though my accomplishments and contacts solidified my social status. This gave me a false sense of self-worth.

Being more concerned with what was on the outside, I lacked true fulfillment on the inside. I disguised my inner void with people, places, and things, ignoring my true problem. By neglecting "self," I encountered my greatest trial. I became the target of an FBI investigation that stripped me of my material wealth, caused me a ton of humiliation, and ultimately gained me a twelve-and a half year prison sentence.

When I stood before the judge and he pronounced the lengthy sentence over my life, I was overtaken with grief. I felt as though my life was over.

In a prison cell, I began to cry out for an understanding. What was the purpose behind my crisis? At my weakest point, I gained my greatest strength! For the first time in my life, I began to shift my focus. In my greatest time of need, I witnessed firsthand how the people whom I admired the most turned against me. I also saw how those who I neglected in the free world, which included my family, turned out to be my greatest supporters.

Alone in my cell, I got a reality check that was greatly needed! You may not be faced with imprisonment, but you may be facing a major illness, the death of a loved one, the loss of a job, a severe financial battle, or some other obstacle that may be hindering you. Whatever your challenge is, I am here to tell you that you can overcome! This trial wasn't sent to kill you. If you choose to, you can find that good that will come out of this situation and allow it to make you stronger, wiser, and better!

During this testing season, you will discover what you are made of. It may be the time you desperately need to work on improving "self." As you change what's on the inside, your situation will ultimately change, too! When the "cake is baked," it is ready to come out of the oven and cool off. However, if the "cake comes out too soon," it will collapse, crumble and be of no good use. Therefore, do not opt to take a shortcut. It will only cause you further havoc! Stay steady and be strong. You were built to outlast the storm!

Overcoming a major obstacle is not an easy task. You will often have to change your mindset and do some rearranging. This will require hard work. But don't worry, your efforts will come with a great reward! Not only will you position yourself to overcome this obstacle, you will be equipped to be victorious in any other challenges you may face in the future.

Right now, you may be asking yourself, "Why me?" But I want you to know there is a bigger picture than what you may currently see. All dilemmas come with an equal opportunity for advancement. Before any major promotion, a test must come. If you are able to pass the test, your greatest victory is just ahead.

We often get discouraged because we are unable to see the opportunity that is disguised within our crisis. In fact, what we view as a headache or a mishap is often actually the doorway into prosperity and purpose. Everyday people pass up on great opportunities because of a lack of accurate perspective. Consequently, many of us have missed out on collecting our "diamonds," or "gems of life," because they weren't presented in a form that we can recognize. This no longer has to be our fate!

It is now time to open our hearts and minds to enter the doorway of wisdom. As we tap into the power of "self," we will be empowered to embrace true spirituality. Entering into this realm, we will no longer view circumstances from a worldly perspective. Instead, we will begin to see life from a clearer point of view. This encounter will help shape our priorities, preventing us from getting caught up in the web of temporary pleasures and superficial happiness. Instead, we will begin to seek true prosperity that has real value.

When we are spiritually whole, the things that once disturbed us will no longer have power. As we learn to develop a shield of protection, we are able to tap into inner peace and joy at any time we desire. I know through my experience that this is a fact!

Even during my imprisonment, I became free and able to sustain my peace. My freedom was no longer based on my outward situation; it became based on my peace within. While incarcerated, I developed endurance by discovering my purpose. I realized I was put on this planet to glorify God by sharing my gifts and talents with others. In prison, I identified those gifts, including learning I had the ability to write. I learned my ministry was one that would help those who were deemed as the underdogs or the forgotten. I would use my personal experiences and my compassion to help uplift these individuals, motivate them to push past their pain and land back on top. As a result of these discoveries, what I perceived to be my worst tragedy turned into my greatest success.

At first, I didn't understand the purpose behind my crisis and desperately wished to avoid it. But, as I yielded to God's divine plan, I discovered there was purpose in my pain. I am no different than you. You, too. can learn to master life's circumstances! You don't have to stay locked behind bars in chains, bound to tribulations.

Equip yourself with wisdom and knowledge and learn how to overcome! There is purpose behind your struggles. Your pain is intended to lead you to ultimate peace and victory! I now invite you to join me on this journey to restoration.

This book was not written to be just read; it was created to be studied. Take your time and go through each section. Stop and meditate on the principles enclosed, especially those in your areas of weakness. Answer the questions at the end of each chapter and share what you learned with someone who may also need this information. As you allow these principles to become one with you, you will be able to apply them naturally in your everyday tasks.

Congratulations! You have taken the first step in your journey to restoration. Stay proactive and continue to fight the good fight of faith! Remember, troubles won't last always. There is a time and a season for all things. This, too, shall pass, but you must be strong! Gird yourself with wisdom and knowledge. And know, you were built to outlast the storm!

I. CHANGING YOUR PERSPECTIVE

POINT 1:

"What I perceive is what I'll receive, so I must take control over what I believe!"

When obstacles occur, it is human nature to panic. After losing our sense of control, we instantly begin to fear the worst is yet to come. Fear is tormenting! Under its harsh clutch, we tend to make choices based on the pressure we feel. Consequently, instead of rationally thinking our decisions through, we become antsy and vulnerable to irrational behavior. This causes us to act based on our emotions rather than the facts. When a crisis or obstacle occurs, we must first stop and take control over our thoughts. The battle begins and ends in the mind.

When I was sentenced to serve twelve and a half years in federal prison, I prayed for my death. The pain and the fear of what was up ahead became unbearable. On top of that, I had no choice but to face my insecurities. Stripped of all the material things that once defined me, in my barest state, I had to face the truth of who I really was.

Trauma for me started at a young age. From as early as I could remember, I realized I was different from many of those around me. As a straight A student in the gifted program, at times, I was the only African American girl in my class. Growing up in the culture of hip-hop music, I aspired to be a "fly" girl, and not a nerd. So, I often tried to cover my intellect by being edgy enough to blend in with the "cool kids."

Gifted also in the arts, I traveled the country as a child actress in an Off-Broadway Play, danced in recitals at Lincoln Center and became a prime attraction in my church's youth choir. From the outside looking in, I achieved success at a young age. However, there was still a void that lingered within.

Although I had cleverly managed to navigate between the intellects, church folks, creatives and the streets, I never felt like I wholly fit into any of these sectors. I was desperately searching for love and affection, and one day I finally thought I found it.

* * *

It was a hot fall day in 1991. I was a proud freshman at Fiorello High School of Performing Arts, aka "The Fame School." As a little girl, I religiously watched the television show. "Fame."

I would dream about dancing down the school hallways like the students in the show. So, when I finally got my acceptance letter, you couldn't tell me anything! For the first time, I was loosened from my mother's tight reigns. She was a schoolteacher who was always home by 3:00 pm, and when she got there I had to be there, too.

Now things were different. I traveled by myself to Manhattan every day from Queens, New York. I had to take a bus and three trains to get to my destination and I loved every minute of the commute. I felt like I was finally growing up and ready to live life to the fullest. Filled with a sense of pride and accomplishment, I met who would soon be my first boyfriend at McDonald's on the way home from school. Immediately, I was attracted to his edge and confidence.

My first love was a sixteen-year-old drug dealer from the 40 Housing Projects in South Jamaica, Queens. It was the peak of the crack cocaine epidemic and my boyfriend and his crew were making tens of thousands of dollars a week. Quickly allured by the culture, he introduced me to the projects and life in the fast lane. Immediately, I was hooked.

I guess it's safe to say that's where this "good girl" went "bad." Rebelling against my mother and the plans she had for me, I was all in. I fell in love, but just as quickly my heart was broken. Giving all of me to this person I thought I'd spend the rest of my life with, I was devastated when he ended up dumping me for the sixteen-year-old girl who was a baker. He said he chose her because she was independent and had her own money. I was heartbroken with no clue how to heal from the fierce pain that stabbed my delicate heart.

Out of impulse and survival, I choose to pursue money at a rapid pace. My mindset was, *no man would ever leave me again because I would have all the money and material things that would protect me from the hurt.* I vowed to never be hurt again.

On first sight, it appeared I had made the right choice. My ambition led me to make millions of dollars. With every dollar I made, I bought things that masked my insecurities. From designer clothes, massive diamond jewelry collections, fleets of luxury cars to estates on the hills, I had it all. I thought these material possesions would finally fill my inner void. To my dismay, it didn't.

Now after all my years of running from the pain, I was trapped in it with no place to go. In a tiny prison cell, I was faced with the reality that all the superficial things I chased, including people, places and things, they all abandoned me. Lost without the material things I used to define my self-worth; I entered a journey of self-exploration. In order to survive the greatest challenge that was ahead of me—my incarceration, I had to dig deep within. The way I took back my power was through my perception. I choose to label my experience as an opportunity to become better. I sat and pondered on ways I could use my time wisely, and instead of mopping and complaining I jumped into action. My first task was building up my spirit to endure. I had to purposely shape my mind to see the good that could come of out my situation. A great shift occurred when I began to do the inner work. Instead of being consumed with the outside, I had to begin to love the image I saw in the mirror.

As I grabbed a hold of my perception, great things begin to happen! Shortly after, I fulfilled my dream of becoming a writer. Researching how to self-publish from prison, I authored over a dozen books and helped several incarcerated women publish their memoirs. My success started in my mind. I saw myself overcoming my obstacle and being successful despite the odds stacked up against me. Then, I turned my thoughts into action and helped others to do the same!

The moral of the story is our thoughts are our power stream! We inevitably receive what we believe. Through the law of attraction, our thoughts become tangible things. Meaning, whatever we concentrate on will ultimately manifest. If our minds are constantly flooded with negative thoughts, by default we will automatically draw negativity into our lives. To have a prosperous life, we must constantly fill our minds with positive thoughts. No matter what comes our way, we can combat negativity by purposefully looking for a positive outcome. Believing in our hearts that "all things will work together for our good," no matter how bad things may seem, will position us to channel positive experiences into our lives. This is the key to overcoming every challenge we face!

There is incredible power that reigns within us.

Our experiences become whatever we project them to be. If we label them as positive, we will experience the good that can come out of them. On the other hand, if we label them as negative, we can expect to encounter bad circumstances. Therefore, through our perception and thoughts, we can ultimately change our lives! It's just that simple!

In this chapter, we will spend time working on changing our perspective. We will learn how to tap into the power of the mind to alter how we view our circumstances. This task will position us to successfully conquer any obstacle we may encounter. Also, we will learn how to discipline our minds to dispel negative thoughts, so they are unable to take root. In addition, we will explore the purpose of obstacles and how they can help us grow. It is human nature to believe we shouldn't have to experience rough times. This belief makes us dread pain and obstacles. Consequently, we tend to do everything humanly possible to avoid trials and tribulations. Yet, what we often fail to realize is that without them, we can't grow. Meaning, without obstacles we will not be promoted to the next level of life.

Trials have a unique purpose. When we overcome life's challenges, we expand our mindset and develop character. Trials force us to view life from a different perspective. As a result, it stretches our thoughts and exposes our strengths and weaknesses. Our strengths propel us to tap into our gifts and talents. Our weaknesses enlighten us on what we need to improve. Discovering our strengths and weaknesses are all a part of the self-discovery process. How will you ever know who you are, if you don't know what you are made of? Trials are sent to expose our character and challenge us to improve. In the midst of fiery obstacles, character is built!

Oftentimes, we measure success according to worldly standards. We falsely believe accomplishments, wealth, and fame determine our self-worth. This mentality causes many to miss out on fulfilling their purpose on earth. You can have all the money in the world, great fame, and tons of accolades under your belt, yet still feel miserable and unfulfilled. That is because each of us are designed to complete a specific task on earth, which is our purpose. Until we complete this assignment, the inner void in our hearts will not be filled. There is no way around it!

Think about it . . . Celebrities and other wealthy people are constantly flooding the news with stories about their mishaps. Like you and I, they strive to receive what they perceive to be ultimate success, only to obtain it and still not find inner fulfillment. Their lives prove that wealth, fame, and fortune alone will not bring us complete satisfaction. In fact, it will do the exact opposite.

Without finding our purpose and completing the assignment God has prepared for us, we will never find ultimate peace. The road to discovering purpose comes with obstacles. As we embrace them, we prepare ourselves to be led into God's ultimate plan for our lives. Now that we know trials and tribulations have a divine purpose, let's further explore the reason behind them. This will help us to endure hardships easier.

I.   *Trials are sent to help us develop character*

Character is not taught, it is learned. Through trials and tribulations, we develop "moral fibers" that keep our lives woven smoothly together. God allows trials to help us prepare for what He desires to give us. Just like parents won't give their ten-year-old child a brand-new car to drive, God will not give us blessings that we are not fully developed to handle.

In order to receive the fullness that God has for us, we must be molded. Trials and obstacles mold us. They increase our knowledge, so we can maintain the gifts the Father desires to give us. As we develop character, we open the doors for blessings to come pouring in! Godly character consists of love, joy, peace, humility, longsuffering, kindness, goodness, faithfulness, gentleness and self-control. These are the attributes we must develop to live a prosperous life, and without them (integrity), the very things we work hard to get can easily be snatched away from us. Godly character protects us from dangerous snares and traps. During trials, we are forced to see the necessity of maintaining good character. As we develop in this area, we are equipped to soar and receive God's best for our lives!

II.   *Trials are sent to make us compassionate toward others*
In the fast-paced world we live in, it's easy to become self-absorbed. Racing to the finish line, we often neglect the needs of others, believing every man should fend for himself. This is not the way God intended for us to be. We were created to be compassionate beings that help one another. God uniquely designed each of us with specific gifts and talents. They are given to us to help serve others, not just ourselves. When we misuse our gifts, we feel empty inside. This particular void signals us that we are not performing in line with our purpose on earth. On the other hand, when we utilize our gifts in alignment with our purpose, God rewards us with peace and inner satisfaction.

   Trials and tribulations help us gain compassion for humanity. When we experience seasons of hardships, we are able to identify and relate to the pain of others, causing us to become more sympathetic. Compassion is sincere concern for another that is heartfelt. It arises from experience. As we suffer hardships, or we watch others we love suffer hardships, it creates great compassion. This cultivates a burning desire within us to help others in need. Often, the very area in our lives that causes us the most pain, becomes the area in which we're most effective with helping others who've experienced a similar hardship.

Therefore, our trials not only cause us to become more compassionate, they also lead us to discovering our purpose. Each of us were placed on this earth to be servants of the Most High God. When we help others, that is our service to God. Many times, we get so caught up with achieving our own goals that we forget to serve or give back. This selfish behavior comes with consequences—we are held stagnant.

According to the law of reciprocity, the more we give, the more we will receive. Look at some of our country's wealthiest people, such as Bill Gates and Oprah Winfrey. They are also the world's biggest philanthropists. They have gained great wealth because they have learned the key to success is giving. The more you give, the more you receive.

Compassionate people are givers! Life's hurdles force us to look into the mirror of compassion. When we experience situations where we are in need, it's easier to recognize the needs of others. Our hearts soften when we are touched by others during our low points. Their kind, compassionate acts become contagious, and we begin to desire to join the great chain of nurturing those in need. When a person exercises their gift of compassion, it invokes effective change in others. It is just that potent!

Before my imprisonment, I thought very little about incarcerated women. I had no clue what they went through and cared very little about their experiences. These women were not my concern, because I was unable to relate or identify with their pain. In the free-world, I concerned myself with chasing wealth and worldly success. It wasn't until I endured my greatest trial, imprisonment, that I began to take notice of the many incarcerated women around me who were in need.

As I suffered hardships, I developed a deep compassion for my peers who needed assistance. My experience led me to become the co-founder of WomenOverIncarcerated, a non-profit organization that provides resources to incarcerated women throughout the country. While behind bars, I also developed the "Voices of Consequences Enrichment

Series," a nondenominational self-help series. This work has helped incarcerated women across the world heal, recognize their potential, and recapture their dreams.

Without my experience, I would not have been moved to action. I had my own plans, but God had a greater plan! As I yielded to His will, my life began to gain meaning, and I received the inner fulfillment I so desperately desired.

I share my story to inspire you to push ahead! Don't allow your obstacles to keep you bound. Know there is purpose in your pain! Yet, it is up to you to take time out to discover the opportunity that lies in the midst of your trial.

III.   *Trials are sent to humble us*

It is human nature to be enthralled by power. We like to be in control. This control often misleads us into believing we can manipulate events at any time to work out in our favor. This simply is not true. God has the final say so over our lives. He determines when we are born and ultimately when we will die. As people become successful, it is natural to become prideful. We become engrossed in what we can do and how we can do it, forgetting the One who gave us the power to perform.

Trials give us a reality check that we are not in charge! They force us to pursue our "Higher Power." Trials guide us back on the correct path and lead us to our knees for guidance. Guidance from our "Higher Power" then propels us back to purpose. Think about how many prestigious people we read about in the newspaper who experience a sudden crisis. One day they are on top of the world, full of great wealth, respect, and esteem. Then suddenly, they fall from the top and become the ridicule of their rivals.

During this period, they felt humiliation that made it seem as though life was over. In this situation they have two options: give up or get back up! Many people give up because they are unable to see the great opportunity that lies in the midst of their crisis.

When a trial is sent to humble you, the best thing to do is to yield to the process. Take a look at yourself. Admit your shortcomings and seek your "Higher Power" for help. God is merciful. Once we get the lesson behind the trial and correct our lives, we are promoted and advanced to the next level. We've passed the test! The greatest victory is the "comeback." When people are able to see you hit rock bottom and rise up again, their respect and esteem for you grows even greater. It exhibits your character and shows what you are made of. Then, it is clearly understood that you did not build your empire on luck, but you are indeed blessed with wisdom and favor from your "Higher Power."

Look at Donald Trump, who many may perceive as one of the most prideful or seemly confident person in the world. At one time, he had it all and lost it. During his season of trials, he was ridiculed and received much humiliation. Many of his peers counted him out! Trump didn't give up; he re-grouped. His trial opened his eyes and gave him a reality check of his life and those around him. This process fueled him with the push he needed to drive him back to the top. Trump performed an amazing comeback! He became greater than he was before he lost it all! His obstacle allowed him to see what he was made of, which ultimately gave him the confidence to become the President of the United States. Whether you care for Trump or not, you can't deny his resilience. It's the obstacles he's encountered that ultimately built his faith.

I can relate. I came home from prison after serving nine years behind bars. Many counted me out. However, I was determined to rise above the challenges I faced. With each victory I gained, I became even more determined. It made me realize with faith and hard work, nothing is impossible. Since that time, I have gone on to do great things. You and I are no different!

The key to overcoming adversity is to learn the lesson behind the trials we face. Then seek wisdom and knowledge to triumph over them. Wisdom is the "what to do" and knowledge is the "how to do it." If you allow it, your greatest obstacle will lead to your greatest discovery. This discovery can only be found when you humble yourself and seek your "Higher Power" for the strategy you need to overcome!

IV.   *Trials lead us to repentance*

When we are high off life, sometimes we become so engrossed in the things of the world, we commit sins that we may not see anything wrong with. It is human nature to be selfish and to concern ourselves with satisfying our flesh. If we get caught up in a worldly lifestyle, we can self-destruct. All sin comes with future consequences!

When we get out of line, God often uses obstacles to draw us back to Him. He allows troubles to arise so we can realize our errors and correct them. Just as a parent punishes his child whom he loves, God punishes us to correct our wrongdoings. The punishments are not sent to kill us; they are sent to lead us into repentance. They help us open our eyes and see life from a different point of view.

When trials come to lead us into repentance, we are to yield and accept responsibility for our wrongdoings. This doesn't have to be a public spectacle. Repentance is personal between us and our "Higher Power." It is admitting we are wrong and making the necessary changes to permanently correct our errors. When we are honest and truly remorseful for our wrongdoings, and make the necessary changes within, we advance to the next level and our obstacle subsides.

During our trials, we must honestly evaluate our lives to detect our wrongdoings. The longer we remain stubborn and refuse to fix "self," the longer we will remain in chaos and confusion. Trials are the periods we use to honestly evaluate "self" and make the necessary changes for improvement. As we make these changes, we grow. As we become better people, we are rewarded for our maturity.

V. *Trials are sent to increase our faith*

It is human nature to remain in our comfort zone. We do not like the unknown, because we like to believe we are in control over life's circumstances. The problem with staying in our comfort zone is, it keeps us from reaching our fullest potential. In this case, God sends trials into our lives so we can increase our faith and soar to levels we never dreamed of, or imagined!

You may have a plan, but God ultimately has a greater plan for you! In order to get you out of your comfort zone, He often sends obstacles in your life to force you to grow and expand your horizons. He is not doing this to hurt you. On the contrary, He is letting these obstacles arise to build you up and make you stronger.

Once you are able to see your strength, your faith increases, which causes an inner desire to excel to higher heights.

Without obstacles, many people accept the status quo of life. They choose jobs, not because they like them or because they are passionate about their careers. Instead, they seek these jobs for safety and security. This is not God's plan. He desires to be our safety and our security.

God desires our work here on earth to be pleasurable. It is up to us to tap into our gifts and pursue careers in the field that line up with our purpose. God gives each of us an inner desire. That desire leads to purpose. When we do the things we love to do, we do them with passion. Even if we aren't paid to do them, we would still do these tasks and enjoy them.

Oftentimes, when God is ready for us to move into our divine assignments, He creates obstacles that force us to operate in faith. Suddenly, you may lose your job and not understand why this is happening, only to finally discover your field of passion. In this case, your struggles and hardships, which are temporary, lead you to a permanent flow of joy and abundance.

Remember, your plans are not God's plans! God's plans are always greater. They are perfect for your life. God does not make mistakes. It is up to us to change our perspective to match God's perspective, so we can see the bigger picture.

Anything we desire to receive in this life we need faith to get it. If we do not believe, we will not receive. Obstacles help us increase our faith. As we overcome our hurdles, we're able to see God's greater plans. This strengthens our belief and desire to achieve.

God wants each of us to believe in His abilities. He sends trials to lead us to Him. As we begin to seek our "Higher Power," He leads and guides us through our dilemmas. The more obstacles we overcome in life, the greater our accomplishments will be here on earth. This increases our faith. Just as we need water to live, we need faith to be successful in life.

VI.   *Trials are sent to bring us into our purpose.*

As we previously discussed, we were all put on this earth to perform a particular task or function. Oftentimes, many of us are clueless of what this task is, so we maintain the status quo. We watch the television, read newspapers and magazines, and observe others around us, then we determine what we will do to become successful. Discovering purpose is an inner work. It does not come from copying those whom society praises. Many people take up trades or pursue careers to please others, only to later discover that they are miserable in their chosen fields.

God gives each of us an inner desire we are supposed to follow. Throughout this journey of overcoming our obstacles, we will constantly discover different attributes of life that will ultimately lead to purpose.

Purpose is very important. Without purpose you cannot live an abundant life! It is vital that you take the time out to discover your purpose. A great book to read to help you find your purpose is, *A Purpose Driven Life* by Rick Warren. Millions of people have tapped into the power of purpose by reading this book. The quicker you discover purpose, the smoother your ride will be through life's obstacle course.

VII. *Trials are sent to get the attention of others around you*

Many of us have moved through life, carrying the weights of others on our shoulders. When we do this, we think we are helping that person, but we are really disabling them. We have done for others the very things they should have done for themselves. As a result, we have helped to hinder them. A person will not progress until they are able to care for themselves. Many of us have blocked our loved ones from their personal growth. If we do not take heed to God's warning signals to move out the way and let that person flourish, He then moves us by some sort of trial or obstacle. In this case, our dilemma forces those around us to step up to the plate and grow!

Often, we are not appreciated until our services are missed. An office manager, or even a secretary, works hard every day and seems to go unnoticed. It's not until they go on vacation or use sick leave that their boss or their co-workers are able to see how important their services are to the company.

At times, the same happens in our personal lives. In that case, God allows us a time out, so those around us can take heed to our importance and our attributes.

It is vital that we set boundaries for ourselves and not allow people to take advantage of us. It is a miserable life taking on the responsibilities of others, which they can do for themselves. That is not fair to you. You must learn to take care of "self," which we will go into further along in this book. Taking care of "self" makes you place your own needs as a priority. If you over work yourself and you are dead and gone, you are of no use to anybody. Therefore, preserve yourself and begin to care for your own needs.

Obstacles that are sent to get the attention of those around you also open your eyes to see where you are overstepping your boundaries. If this occurs, take heed and change your course of action. Allow others to grow by removing yourself as their aid so they may become responsible for themselves! Take a time out to discover what you have been neglecting from "self," by taking care of someone else's responsibilities. When you work on "self" and change your course, your obstacles will start to subdue.

In this chapter, we have been enlightened to the many reasons trials occur in our lives. Now that we understand that our trials have a purpose, we know they are sent to help advance, not to destroy us. The sooner we take heed to the lesson, the quicker we're able to get through the trial. When you view your obstacles as having purpose, they are in fact no longer obstacles at all. Instead we view them as opportunities!

The hardest thing at times is to admit there is a need for change. Oftentimes, we avoid all the signs until we run into a major obstacle. Now looking back, I realize prison was the place God used to save me. In the world, I had been so busy doing things my way that I didn't realize I had been prostituting my anointing. I had many gifts and talents, yet I was using them for my own purpose. Prison was a humbling experience. It made me acknowledge that I needed God and I was not in control as I thought. In a dark place, I got to know God for myself.

In the past, I had relied on my pastor, my parents or my grandparents' experiences with God. But now I had my own. Not only did this experience build my character and increase my faith, I was led to discover my purpose. My outreach ministry started in prison. In fact, it became my residency training. I gained compassion for incarcerated women and those who face challenges. It led me to create books and programs to help others shift their mindset and heal. Without this experience I would not have the qualifications or desire to do what I do today. What I perceived to be my downfall was actually a stepping stool to my future destiny.

Could you imagine if I would have given up? I contemplated suicide several times. But, thank God, something inside wouldn't allow it to happen. Today, I stand whole! Who would have thought the prisoner would be released and several major networks would tell my story in feature films? Who would have thought I would travel the world speaking at prestigious colleges and places such as center stage at Essence Festival? And who would have thought that I would be called on by distinguished elected officials and leaders of prominent organizations to create books and programs that would help hundreds of thousands of people? Undoubtedly, I didn't see the full picture.

However, when I changed my perception of how I viewed my obstacle, ultimately, I changed my life! You, too, have the same choice!

Now that your perspective is clearer, take a time out and think about how you previously viewed your obstacle. Then, re-evaluate your view based on what you have now learned. Deeply think about what reason may closely fit with your dilemma and think about what good can come out of your situation. Spend time meditating on those thoughts.

When you come to a positive conclusion about what you stand to gain from your current situation, I want you to say this affirmation "I no longer view my obstacle as an obstacle, for it is not an obstacle at all. My situation is an opportunity for growth and advancement. Therefore, I will embrace this opportunity and triumph over all difficulties that come my way. As I do, I will be rewarded! I know that God loves me, and He will never put more on me than I can bear. God's only desire is to make me greater and stronger. I thank Him for the opportunity to grow. I know I was built to outlast the storm, so this season too shall pass! And abundance, peace, happiness, and joy are mine. I claim it, so I will obtain it!"

Congratulations! You have completed the first step in our journey to overcome! Now that you have changed your perspective, it will be easier to weather the storm. Continue along this process so you can further position yourself to win. You've got this!

QUESTIONS

1. What are the major reasons trials are sent?
2. Why must we change our perspective about our trials?
3. Why must we seek to discover our purpose?
4. Why do people reach major heights of accomplishment and wealth, yet are still unfulfilled?
5. How do trials help us?

WRITING ASSIGNMENT

Describe your current obstacle and what is making it difficult to bear. Then explain the good or opportunity you believe can come out of this challenge.

II. PARTNERSHIP WITH YOUR "HIGHER POWER"

POINT 2:

"When the storm comes, I need a safety tower, so I reach out to my "Higher Power.""

When the judge banged the gavel and stated, "You are hereby sentenced to serve 151 months in prison," life as I knew it changed. At first, I humbly cried out to God for help, hoping the nightmare I experienced would quickly end. After reality settled in, and I realized I was stuck, I began to question God. For years, I had been seeking Him for answers through people. I had everyone I thought who had a special relationship with God to pray for me. I had given hundreds of thousands of dollars to various churches and was even credited with helping to fund a mini-cathedral for one of the ministries I frequented most often.

If I could buy my way out of prison, I had all the bases covered, or so I thought. Especially since all the prophets, ministers, evangelists, and even priests, who collected my money said I was not going to prison. They told me I just had to use my faith to push through and when I finally went to court, I'd be released.

Taking their beliefs as the Gospel, I was devastated to the core to learn their words were untrue. Even more hurtful, after my tithes and offerings stopped, they stopped their prayers, too. No more phone calls, letters or acknowledgements. Instead, I was abandoned and forgotten and that was a double stab to my open wounds.

As the days began to go by, not only did I begin to question leadership in the church and their motives, I started questioning God. Was He really real? And, did prayer actually work? Or, was God a fairytale people told to control us. I debated heavily in my mind. "If God is such a good God, why would he allow me to suffer so much?" I asked myself over and over as I sobbed behind the dingy prison blankets, which I used to cover my tears. It was all confusing and I had no one to explain the things we are going to discuss in this chapter.

I know how it feels to appear to be forgotten, especially when you see so many others around you being blessed. I just want to assure you that God is a good God, whether it feels like it or not. And as you continue through this journey, you will learn ALL things will work together for your good! It did for me!!

Obstacles are often sent to bring us to our knees. When challenges arise that are too great for us to solve in our own strength, we come to the realization that we need help. When this occurs, God wants us to seek Him for assistance, rather than man. Obstacles are God's roll call to get our attention. He desires for each of us to spend time with Him and get to know the truth of His greatness.

It is human nature to get so caught up in the events of life and achieving success that we forget our Creator. Without Him, life wouldn't be possible at all! There is no success unless God grants it!

God wants us to take pleasure in the things He allows us to obtain or experience, but we should never put creations before the Creator. This is a mistake many of us make. Anything we put before God becomes an idol. This can be a job, an accomplishment, an item, or even someone we love. It's easy to unconsciously fall victim to creating false idols. Therefore, it's a good practice to constantly evaluate our lives and make sure we don't allow anything within God's creation to become our idols.

When we put people, places, and things before God, He allows obstacles to occur to get our attention and bring us back on course. Our dilemmas remind us that we need a Power greater than ourselves to survive. When we come to the realization that we need God's help to make it through life's trials, and we can't make it on our own, we arrive at the point of surrender. To surrender is simply to come to God and acknowledge that we need His help.

Surrendering, for many people, is a difficult thing to do. Humans instinctively have a stubborn nature. We want to believe we are in control and have power over everything. Sudden disasters and chaos allow us to see clearly that we are not in control; God is! When we surrender to God, we open the doors to receive His help and guidance.

Spirituality is a personal choice. Each of us has our own personal belief system of who God is to us. This book was not created to change your perspective of God as you view Him. This book was written to help you acknowledge your need of your "Higher Power" to make it through rough seasons in life. If we have no power over life or death, over the sun or the moon, or over the storms and the rain, we know there is a force that exists, which is greater than both you and me.

From the beginning of time, people have experienced obstacles and have overcome them by seeking God's assistance. Just as they triumphed, we can too! The key to this journey is seeking the assistance of our "Higher Power."

When storms suddenly arise, we are not to panic, or even seek people. The first thing we are to do is seek refuge in the tower of our "Higher Power." That's where we receive peace, comfort, and knowledge to overcome.

When hardships occur, we are to surrender to God and admit that we need His help. When we surrender, we open the doors to create a relationship with Him. God doesn't want us to travel through life alone. He wants to be our Partner. What greater Partner can we obtain than the One who created the heavens and the earth? When we take God on as our Partner, His strength becomes our strength, and His abilities become our abilities. We can do all things with God! There is no problem too hard for Him to solve!

In order to take God on as our Partner, we have to develop a relationship with Him. Just as a human partner, we must discover what He likes and His concerns. As we spend time getting to know God, we learn His ways. Then He begins to reveal His plans and His purpose for our lives. We can talk to God just as we talk to a friend. God is interested in the matters that concern us. When we talk to God about our problems, we invite Him in to help us.

God is a Gentleman! He doesn't push His agenda on us. He reveals His agenda, then it is up to us to decide to embrace His plan. God will not become our Partner and interfere with our affairs, unless we allow Him to do so. We allow God in our lives by maintaining communication with Him. This communication is called prayer.

Prayer doesn't have to be formal or elegant. All we have to do is open up our mouths and be sincere. Tell God our concerns, and He will provide the solutions. God wants to know we trust and depend on Him. Our trials are sent to test our belief. God wants to see just what you will do! Will you run to man, or will you run to Him? God sits back and waits for each one of us to realize we do indeed need His assistance. When we come to God, He is ready and able to help us.

Even though our stormy seasons may seem lonely, I am here to tell you, you are never alone! God is with you at all times! Friends and family members may leave you or forsake you, but God will never leave you alone. Some of us have been betrayed by people, and this betrayal hurt us as if we had been stabbed with a knife! We blamed the people who betrayed us, but we seldom realized it was all in God's plan! He allowed the betrayal to occur to show us that we don't need these people. There is indeed a lesson in the pain.

God uses vessels on this earth to help us. Some people come for a season, some come for a reason and others are there for a lifetime! God uses people for His own purpose. We are never to rely on people; we are only to rely on God. There will be seasons in our lives where God allows us to be separated from people, so our attention can be focused solely on Him. When we seek God and not people, we pass the test, and our obstacles subside.

God is in control over all life's events. Anything that happens, He has allowed it! It is up to us to seek our "Higher Power" for an interpretation of what is happening and what we need to do. All problems come with a solution. God gives us wisdom and knowledge to solve our problems. Wisdom is the "what to do" and knowledge is the "how to do it." Wisdom and knowledge both come by first seeking God, then asking Him to guide us to the solution.

Often when we ask God for the solution, He sends it to us in forms that may appear to be disguised, or unfamiliar. It's up to us to sift through the instruments He shows us and search for the solution. Seek and you will ultimately find! When we learn to search for wisdom, we advance as people. God wants us to be knowledgeable and self-sufficient. Therefore, obstacles force us to grow. They stretch us to tap into the power that lies dormant within us.

In order to overcome our obstacles, we must remain open minded. We cannot box God in. He has a purpose and a reason for all things. In prayer we are to ask God to help us view our situations from His perspective and show us His perfect plan for our lives. When we do, He will show us the route which is best for us to take.

Without our "Higher Power," we will remain lost and in darkness. Common wisdom is not enough to overcome. As we seek God's help, He also strengthens us, giving us the ability to sustain through the storm. God knows our needs, and as we seek Him, He makes our burdens lighter. God will provide us with all the key essentials to become victorious.

God is the One who sends us people, places, and things. They are gifts from Him. If someone exits your life, do not worry! Just as God sent them, He has the ability to send someone else! Take your concerns to God in prayer and watch Him open supernatural doors of provision! Always remember, God is your provider, not people. Even if a person blesses you, it is God who provided the blessing. You are to be grateful to people for following God's instructions, but you are not to rely on them. Your complete trust and reliance must be in your "Higher Power." God is the only One who gives you the power to get wealth and the power to sustain it, not man!

Throughout life, many of us have experienced great tragedies and tribulations. Because we did not understand the purpose, or God's intention for the trial, many of us have become angry with God. We blame Him consciously or subconsciously for our mishaps. It's a common question when obstacles occur: "If God loves me and if He is a good God, why would He allow this happen to me?" This type of thinking causes bitterness and blocks our communication with God, which ultimately blocks our blessings.

It is important to always remember God does not make mistakes! What we think is a tragedy could actually be a blessing. Our perception of our obstacles must be correct. If not, we could miss the plan of God for our lives.

Some people get angry with God when they lose their loved ones. We feel as though God shouldn't have taken this person away from us. It is important to be open-minded and unselfishly analyze our hardships. When our loved ones pass on who had a correct relationship with their "Higher Power," they go to a better place. We have no clue what suffering they may have had to endure on earth while they were here. Yes, we miss them and wish they were around for support, yet their light still shines bright in our hearts. One day we will meet them again on better terms. When we truly love someone, we want what's best for them. God is the only One who knows what's best.

Instead of being angry with God, we must surrender. When we surrender our own will and accept God's will, life takes on a new meaning. Things becomes easier because we are no longer fighting against God's plan and purpose. When we surrender, we learn to embrace God's plan. Whatever comes our way, we stand, seek God for guidance and provision and become determined to make it through. Instead of murmuring and complaining and labeling our obstacles as tragedies, we stand firmly knowing something good MUST come out of this situation. Then we pray to our "Higher Power" and ask Him to reveal His goodness and mercy to us by showing us the benefits and purpose of our journey. Remember, God is just. All things, no matter how bad they seem, will work together for our good!

Developing a good partnership takes time. You have to get to know and trust your partner and develop a relationship. This can only be done by spending time and getting to know each other. We learn about God by reading about Him. Each of us have our own belief system of God, which is translated in writings enclosed in a Holy Book.

If we desire to get God's attention, we must learn what He likes. It's just like a man trying to get the attention of a woman and he finds out she likes pink roses, so he sends them to her. The woman becomes elated and decides to pay the man some attention. It is no different with God. He desires each of us to get to know Him. When we read our Holy Book, we learn the character of God and what He likes. We discover stories about others who have experienced similar challenges.

We learn what they did to gain God's attention, and we see how God brought them through. These stories and passages inspire us to do the same things these people did to get God's attention, and they give us divine strategies, while building inner strength. Ultimately, they pick up our spirits and give us the courage and the faith we need to move forward.

Reading my Bible daily while incarcerated saved my life. Every word I read gave me the will power I needed to push on. I compared my situation to the challenges of other characters such as Daniel, Joseph and Job. When I saw what God brought them through, it reassured me that He would bring me out of bondage too!

It is ideal to give our "Higher Power" the first portion of our day. This will give us the strength and insight we need to have a productive day. Therefore, before we start our daily activities, we should spend time with our Creator and give Him thanks for allowing us to make it to see another day. During this time, we should also read some sort of scripture, affirmation or meditation that helps us get to know more about the attributes of God. By doing this we intake our daily spiritual food.

Just as we need physical food to live, we need spiritual food to charge our spirits, giving us the power to move on. The more time we spend with God, the more strength we will have to jump over life's hurdles. It is during our worship and fellowship with God where we increase our faith. It is the key ingredient we need to stand when life's obstacles flood us. Faith comes by hearing, and hearing by the word of God. Whenever you feel down or discouraged, regenerate your spirit by reading or listening to God's word!

When we are interested in taking up a trade or learning a new skill, we seek out others who are experienced in this field to teach us. We can use the same strategy to develop a closer relationship with God. Find a comfortable place of worship and go there to learn more about God. When we spend time with other believers, we strengthen our own faith. We learn strategies and techniques from them that help us in our walk with God. Believers can also help influence us to stay on the right track or warn us when we are headed in the wrong direction. In essence, these people become our accountability partners. Once we find a *trusted* place of worship, we can go there to seek refuge during times of tribulation. In these places, the faces of those we fellowship with can help strengthen our spirits and give us the endurance we need to push ahead.

Some of us have several questions and even suspicions about God and religion. This keeps us from moving forward into a relationship with God. Many have often asked the question: "Is God really real?" If you are one of those who feel this way, pray and ask God to reveal Himself to you. The only way to get to know God is to invite Him into your life. God is all knowing. Try Him! Talk to Him in prayer as you would talk to your closest friend. Tell Him just how you feel. Let Him know your concerns and most importantly, ask for His guidance. He will help you!

Prayer is one of the most powerful forms of receiving help. Since the beginning of times, billions of people have prayed and seen miraculous results. Unexplainable miracles have occurred shortly after prayer, and it has been proven! We can obtain these same results. All we have to do is pray and believe, and ultimately, we will receive.

Additionally, prayer without faith, or belief, is void. It will not produce results! When we pray to our "Higher Power," we must believe He hears us and will answer us. When we pray with faith it ignites power. Our communication reaches God rapidly and moves Him to do something about our problems.

Many of us fail to receive help from God because we fail to pray. It's like the old saying, "A closed mouth doesn't get fed!" If you want help from God, you have to open your mouth, request help, and believe you'll receive the answer. A good way to increase your faith and expectancy during prayer is to start giving God thanks for what you prayed for, even before you receive it. As you begin to give God thanks, you open your spirit to believing your answer is on the way. Faith is the key ingredient that gets God's attention.

As you thank God, you are saying to Him, "God, I trust you and I know you have already answered my request." Thanking God in advance is speaking life into your request. It's your special announcement to your spirit and the universe that you know your blessing is on the way!

Many of us make the mistake of only seeking God when times are rough. How would you feel if you had a friend you truly loved, who only comes to you when they are in trouble? You know all about that person, yet they have taken little to no time out to get to know you. Numerous times you have helped them out. You have even set up situations where they continuously benefit, yet this person appears to be ungrateful. You only see them or hear from them when things get rough. How would you feel toward them? . . . The same way you would feel about this person is how God feels when we neglect Him.

God should never be used as a quick fix! The more we neglect God, the more obstacles we will undergo! Through our most trying situations, He will force us to see that we need Him, and we can't make it without Him. It is a terrible thing to fall into the hands of an angry God! Save yourself the trouble and make God your Friend and Partner. Seek Him through the good times so life will get even better. And, seek Him through the bad times, so the rough seasons of life quickly pass away.

Develop your own relationship with God so you can count on Him to help you in times of need. Think about the difference between asking a stranger or someone you barely know for help or asking for help from your best friend. When you have established a relationship with your best friend, it is easy to go to him or her in need, and he or she will respond because of their established history with you. It is the same with God. The deeper and closer our relationship becomes with Him, the easier it is to get Him to respond on our behalf. What greater benefit is it than to have a close relationship with the Creator of the entire universe?

Shame and guilt because of our past acts often keep us away from God. We believe we are not good enough to ask Him for help. Always remember, God is a merciful God. He knew when He created us that we would make mistakes. God doesn't intend for us to be perfect, just as a parent doesn't believe his child will always do the right thing. God just wants to know that when we do fall short, we know how to apologize and ask for forgiveness. Developing a relationship with God doesn't mean you have to become a saint over night! That is not realistic. God wants you to be real with Him. Tell Him your faults and ask Him for strength to overcome them. No matter how many times you mess up or fall short, if you ask God to forgive you, and you are sincere, He will help you!

I understand the ravaging, fearsome power of shame and guilt. I beat myself up for endless days for my actions that lead to my incarceration. Every time I saw my children on a prison visiting floor, and tears filled their eyes as they departed, these powerful emotions piled up. It came a point where they began to cripple me. Then, I heard the voice of the Lord in my inner spirit say, "Jamila, I forgave you, so why do you choose to not forgive yourself?"

This experience made me think. If I keep living in the past, I will handcuff myself to all my past pain and trauma. Freedom is forgiveness. It is liberation. It is understanding as humans we all make mistakes. Understanding this truth, I decided to take back my freedom by forgiving myself. What came next was epic! I surrendered my will and allowed God to lead and He turned my tragedy into triumph!

Once we take on God as our Partner and develop a relationship with Him, our burdens become lighter! That which we held onto and tried to figure out for ourselves, we no longer have to carry. We simply ask our Partner for help and leave it up to Him to provide the solution.

When God is your Partner, He gives you inner peace. You no longer have to spend your life being fearful of tomorrow. You no longer have to worry or doubt if you will make it. God will give you peace and assurance that He's going to make everything all right! Through each and every dilemma of your life, God will show Himself faithful.

Now that you understand the benefit of taking God on as a Partner, the only thing left to do is make a choice. Do you want to continue living life in constant chaos or confusion, or do you want to lighten your load and receive the peace of God? The final choice is up to you!

If you have decided you want to take God on as your Partner, please follow me in this short prayer: "God, today, I have come to the realization that I need Your help. I no longer want to go through life carrying these heavy weights on my shoulders. God, I surrender, and I request Your help. I ask You today to become my Partner. Help me to do what I cannot do in my own strength. Give me Your divine wisdom and knowledge, so I will know what to do and how to do it in every aspect of my life.

Strengthen me and give me the faith I need to make it through this journey. Lead me and guide me into Your perfect plan and purpose for my life. Give me the desire to know You more intimately. Reveal Yourself to me, teach me Your ways and show me Your attributes. Forgive me for anything I have done in my past that has not been pleasing to You. Illuminate those things that You desire me to change. Allow me to feel Your love and affection and show me Your favor.

"Today, I know I'm not alone, for You are here with me. Today, I declare You are my Partner, so I believe You will lead me and guide me each day. Before I move forward into life's journey, I will consult you for Your advice.

"Now, I take this moment to declare that You are my Provider. Provide me with the provisions I need to accomplish my purpose on earth. Protect me from evil and close doors that will lead to my destruction. Align me with the right people, places, and things at the correct timing, so I will be successful in all my ventures. Watch over me all the days of my life, as I forever make you my God and my Partner. I thank You now for help and provision. Amen."

Congratulations! You have taken a major step! You are no longer alone in this journey. You now have a faithful Partner who you can forever depend upon!

Don't take this partnership for granted. Create and develop your relationship with God. Honor it because it is sacred. When times get rough, your partnership will sustain you. God will warn you when troubles are ahead, and He will become your tower of refuge!

Today, you have taken up your most powerful defense! You are surely going to make it. With God there is no way you can fail! Reread this chapter and think about ways you can develop a stronger partnership with your "Higher Power."

Remember. You must spend time with God daily to sustain your partnership, even if it's only a few moments. Put God first and watch how quickly you will overcome any hurdle that stands in your way! God bless, you are indeed a champion!

QUESTIONS

1. Why is your partnership with your "Higher Power" important?
2. How do you communicate with your "Higher Power?"
3. In what ways can you develop a closer relationship with God?
4. What is faith and why do you need it?
5. What are some of the main reasons people get angry with God?
6. Why is giving God thanks powerful?
7. How does shame and guilt stop us at times from seeking our "Higher Power?" Why is this dangerous?

WRITING ASSIGNMENT

Create a daily schedule for spending time with God. Describe the ways and steps you will take to develop a closer relationship with Him. Include your goals for obtaining a solid partnership. Then, write a letter addressed to your new Partner. Explain your current dilemmas and what you would like Him to assist you with. Also talk to Him in your letter about your new partnership agreement. Tell Him what you desire from this new relationship, as well as what you will contribute. Sign this letter and place it inside your Holy Book. You will be amazed how quickly God honors your request!

III. TAKING TIME OUT TO MEDITATE

POINT 3:

"I can change my course, it's never too late!
But, first, I must stop and meditate."

When problems arose in my life, the first thing I would do is panic and call a friend. I can't tell you how many bad decisions I've made under pressure, including choosing the wrong mate, impulse shopping and getting myself into agreements that later haunted me. Consequently, my actions led to more problems, endless sleepless nights, pain and agony, all leading to anxiety and depression. Had I understood the importance of meditation and how to do it, I could have saved myself years of pain. That's why this chapter is significantly important to me!

In the last chapter, we learned that when problems occur, we are to first stop and seek the assistance of our "Higher Power." After we pray, the second step is to stay still and be quiet so we can receive the answer to our prayer request. We receive our answers to life's problems when we meditate.

Meditation is simply closing our eyes and focusing on our "Higher Power." We close our minds to all outside influences, and we look to our "Higher Power" to provide us with the solution. At times, we make bad decisions and wrong choices because we fail to ask God for help, and we don't wait on Him to send us the answer.

God talks to us frequently, but we are often unable to hear Him. God speaks to us by sending still, subtle thoughts into our minds. If our minds are busy racing with fear, worry, and doubt, we will miss God's voice. In that case, God's directions are blocked by other negative thoughts.

When we maintain a quiet and meditative state, we allow God to inject His desired plans into our thoughts. The only way to hear from God after we pray is to be quiet and meditate!

As challenges occur, the key to overcoming is to focus on the solution and *not* the problem. We now have our "Higher Power" as our Partner. He promised to provide us with a road map to get us through our obstacles and lead us on the path of purpose. Therefore, we are comforted. If troubles arise, we now know God has allowed it. He knows the purpose for each test and trial. When we stop and consult our Partner, He guides us in the way we should go.

Spending time with God also includes meditation. When we pray, we talk to God; when we meditate, He talks back to us. We need both prayer and meditation to create a perfect union with our Partner. One will not work without the other! God wants us to talk to Him. He also desires to talk to us. Prayer and meditation are our channels to receive awesome results!

Meditation is often viewed as an intricate procedure. People take classes and spend many years trying to figure out how to meditate and commune with God. Meditation does not have to be difficult. Simply quiet your mind and take your thoughts off everything but God. Picture yourself sitting at God's throne awaiting Him to answer your request. Don't try to figure out your solution on your own, wait for God to tell you what to do. After you pray, ask Him to talk to you and give you guidance. At first, it may take you a little time to spiritually connect, but as you focus on God and His greatness, you will tap into the Source of solution.

God has been waiting to talk to you, but He can't until you quiet your spirit. During meditation, picture your "Higher Power" taking all of your burdens away. See yourself being restored by God's touch. Allow yourself to experience the joy and fulfillment of your prayers being answered. Fill yourself up with gratitude and the same feelings you get when you receive the news that your problem is solved. When you do this, you will expedite your prayer request. Remember, God responds to faith!

The key to meditation is tapping into your inner source of peace. You must learn how to tap into the inner source that sparks joy, no matter what you are encountering. During meditation, don't get caught up in the "what if." Instead, focus on the now. Let nothing else matter except the moment you are in. At this moment you are happy because you are in union with your "Higher Power." In this space you have peace, joy, and assurance that all things in your life will work together for your good. Knowing that God loves you and He cares, give Him all your heavy burdens. He will make a way!

As you release your problems to God, you will feel a sense of peace that will overtake your whole being. Your attitude will change, and depression and worry will turn into gratitude. As you feel this peace, recap all the good things in your life that you are grateful for. Start giving God thanks for these things. God loves an attitude of gratitude, and He honors it! As you become full of thanksgiving, you open the doors for God to bless you even more. It also makes us recount all the ways God has come through for us in our past, which increases our faith and assurance that He will indeed help us once again!

The moment obstacles occur, it is crucial that we take control of our thoughts. Our opposition, which is the enemy of our souls, will always attempt to send us negative thoughts of fear, worry, and doubt. His goal is to cause panic, so we'll act irrationally. We take back our power when we control our thoughts!

According to the universal law of attraction, whatever we think about and concentrate on, we will ultimately manifest. For example, you wake up late and rush to get dressed. Then you spill coffee all over your clothes, and you lose even more time. Irritated by the current events, you change clothes and storm out the door. You tell yourself, "Today is going to be a bad day." Then suddenly, you discover your tire is low. You stop at the gas station to get air, and you realize you left your important papers at home while you were rushing. Everything throughout the rest of that day goes haywire. Why? According to the law of attraction, your negative thoughts attracted more negative experiences. Understanding this truth, it is important that we start our day by cleansing our minds of all negativity.

As we discussed in the last chapter, one of the best things you can do to ensure a peaceful, pleasant day is to start your day by spending time with your "Higher Power."

After you complete your daily spiritual meditations, visualize yourself successfully accomplishing your tasks throughout the day. Go over what you need to do and exactly what you want to see accomplished. As you meditate on these events, you are sending your Partner, which is your "Higher Power," your request.

Your meditative thoughts are saying, "Dear God, this is what I would like to accomplish today. I know you will guide me, protect me, and help me in my pursuit."

I can't stress enough how visualization has helped me. On my prison bunk I would use this method to escape my current state and enter into a sanctuary of peace. Not only did visualizing the life I wanted bring me instant joy, it also gave me the will power to push ahead and make my dreams my reality. You can do the same!

As you ask God for help, you essentially clear the pathway of negativity and open the doorway to your success. That is why it is crucial to meditate!

The mind is very powerful! Every battle begins and ends with the mind. The mind dictates our views. It prejudges our experiences. It can make them more difficult or easy to endure. What we receive is ultimately a matter of choice. What do you choose to believe?

As we discussed, we all have an enemy of opposition that stands in the way of our destiny. The enemy's greatest attack is orchestrated in the mind. He knows if he can get us to accept the negative thoughts he sends, ultimately that will become our experience. Consequently, the enemy sends us thoughts of fear, worry, and doubt. If we are not in alignment with our "Higher Power" and "self," we begin to believe these thoughts are in fact our own. Think about it . . . You can be somewhere enjoying yourself, and out of nowhere a thought pops into your mind that you were not previously thinking. Then, it suddenly reoccurs with other strong negative thoughts. This is how the enemy works! He bombards our minds with negative thoughts that overwhelm us and influence us to react based on our emotions.

An acronym for Fear is **F**alse, **E**vidence, **A**ppearing, **R**eal. You must remember, fear is based on fiction! It's like walking through a haunted house and getting scared when the ghost actor jumps out. It is all an illusion! The sound effects, the costumes, and the props are strategically built to deceive you. This is the same as the enemy's plan. Remember, fear is **f**alse **e**vidence **a**ppearing **r**eal! When troubles arise, do not allow fear to take hold of you. If you do, you sign for the package. Don't sign for it! Instead, immediately take a time out and clear all negative thoughts. Consult your "Higher Power" in prayer, then meditate and await the solution.

Feelings are our indicators that signal the types of thoughts we allow to occur in our minds. Our minds are constantly moving, picking up many different thoughts. At times, we are unaware of what we are allowing ourselves to think about. When we start to feel negative vibes of anxiety, depression, or fear, that is our indicator that we must change our thoughts! Meditation and prayer unlocks your secret closet of escape.

Prayer does not only have to be spoken; you can make your prayer request to your "Higher Power" by simply speaking to Him through your thoughts. It is very powerful when you use visualization in your prayers. See your "Higher Power" helping you in your mind. Visually see yourself being restored. Stop and feel the feelings of restoration, just as if they were occurring in real time. When you learn to master the technique of visualization through prayer, your experience will become reality.

The key to a peaceful life is learning how to make positive thinking a lifestyle. It is human nature to become worried and fearful when troubles occur. In order to change our lifestyle, we must change our habits. A habit is learned behavior. Habits can be picked up in as little as two to three weeks. Whatever we train and program ourselves to do, becomes our habits.

Peaceful living begins with making positive thinking a habit. At first this task may not be easy. We discussed previously that feelings are our radar and signals of the thoughts we are experiencing. Therefore, we must get in tune with "self," by constantly examining ourselves to determine just what we are thinking about. If not, our minds will move ahead of us and program themselves as they wish. We must make it a habit to counteract all negative thoughts. We accomplish this task by exchanging our negative thoughts with positive thoughts.

In this chapter, we will learn multiple techniques to change our thought process through various forms of meditation. Remember, meditation is our outlet of release from daily trials and tribulations. Through meditation we can sustain our peace no matter what we undergo. It's important that you internalize these techniques and utilize them! Do them continuously until you make them a habit! If you apply them correctly, they can increase your quality of life substantially!

Utilizing affirmations is a technique that helps manage your thoughts. Affirmations are positive statements that describe our intentions. For example, "I am successful. Today, I will make it. I possess the strength to overcome."

It is a good idea to speak life over our situations by using positive words. The tongue is very powerful! By constantly saying what we want and believing it, we can achieve it! We send a powerful message into the universe, causing our desires to come to pass. That is why it is dangerous to speak negativity against ourselves. For example, many people often say things like, "I can't do this. All I'm going to ever experience is problems. My life is a mess." By speaking these negative words over our lives, we send a signal to the universe that this is what we desire to be our experience.

If you want to be successful, you must govern the words you speak! Do not let negative statements come out of your mouth! Regardless of how you feel, speak positive words, and watch your experiences line up with your verbal request.

When you are experiencing challenges in life, or you wish to move to another level in your journey, take the time out to figure out just what you want to experience. Write out your desires, and then turn them into affirmations. Even your everyday goals can be converted! For example, "Today, I will be successful in every venture I undergo. I will spend time with my 'Higher Power.' I will take time out to care for 'self.'"

You can also create long-term goals and speak them in the present tense. For example, "I am successful. I am rich in spirit and in wealth. I have everything I need. I am always happy because I know God loves me." In this format, you are speaking into existence what you desire.

It's so many days I had to use my words to swiftly shift my state of despair. When the enemy tries to take me off course and put thoughts in my mind, I talk back! That's how I fight! I use my words to defend me. Through my biggest battles, I learned to become my biggest coach. I do that by talking myself into action!

"Jamila, you got this! Jamila, you are wonderfully made in God's image. There is no battle you can't overcome. All things are working out for your good. There is a reward at the end of this journey. Just push!"

As we continuously speak affirmations on a regular basis, we tell our subconscious mind that these things belong to us! Affirmations help build up our strength, faith, and self-esteem. When we use them in meditation, these words become our mind's road map. It sets the precedence for the thoughts we allow to take place. As we repeatedly say them, these words eventually become one with us, spiritually aligning us to receive our request.

There is power in affirmations! Use this technique to your advantage. On a daily basis, start your day by reciting the affirmations that fit your circumstance. For example, "Today will be a good day because I'm taking charge of it! I refuse to let any negativity take root in my day. My mind is cleansed and renewed. I feel happy and vibrant. I will let my light shine brightly and take charge of this day."

Another good technique to bring you into a peaceful state is to *recount the good times* you have experienced in the past. Recounting the good times can quickly help you ease your mind from negativity.

Just as you can open your favorite digital platform and put it on a particular selection that you like, you should also be able to go into meditation and remember an event that was special and memorable. When you are experiencing rough times, it is vital to recount powerful, memorable moments. This act can instantly help change your entire mood!

When you recount your past, reach deep into your imagination and relive those moments you enjoyed. Just as a movie replays, rewind your good experiences in your mind. See the details in your surroundings and most importantly, feel the feelings you felt at that moment. If you allow yourself to tap into your memory box of positive emotions, you can learn to overpower any negativity that comes your way. Remember, stay in the moment and live it! You have the control over how long your positive emotions in this moment will last. Use it to its fullest potential!

Again, store in your memory bank several experiences that made you feel good. Then, you can go back to them anytime you are in need of feeling those positive feelings again. Music is also helpful to remember good times. When things aren't going your way, it's always relaxing to throw in a music recording that you remember hearing during a special moment, or that helps you recount memorable moments.

The Bible says in *Philippians 4:8*, "Whatever things are true, whatever things are noble, whatever things are just, whatever things are pure, whatever things are lovely, whatever things are of good report, if there is any virtue and if there is anything praiseworthy, meditate on these things." We can take this strategy and use it in our meditation.

Each of us have different goals, beliefs, and dreams. We hold the power to get a taste of these experiences in our time of meditation. During meditation, you can do or become anything you like! The key is to tap into your heart's desires and live the experience first in your mind. What makes you happy, or what will make you happy? Whatever it is, ponder on these things. When you do, it will automatically take you into a peaceful, joyous state.

Many of us wish to expand our wisdom and knowledge, so we read. After you read, it is a good practice to stop and meditate and take in the good thoughts which you have learned. This is a very powerful technique which can help you increase your understanding.

After you read your Holy Book, it is also essential to ponder on the words you have read. When you meditate on those powerful words, they become life, sparking faith to arise from within.

In life it is common to become busy. We want everything to happen quickly, so we often miss the nuggets of wisdom that lie within our experience. By pondering, we can recap our day and focus on the lessons that came out of our experiences. Therefore, it is a good practice at the end of each day to sit and meditate on all that has occurred, both good and bad things. Contemplate on ways you can fix those things that occurred that you didn't like, and how you can capitalize off the good experiences. Then, go back in your mind and replay the event as you would have liked to see it play out. This will help change your future interactions.

When we ponder during meditation, it helps us come up with creative solutions. Our minds are clear and focused, so we can make discoveries we could not have made with our minds being bombarded with multiple thoughts. In essence, we make meditation our lab where we fix and adjust those things that need our attention.

Pondering is a powerful tool. It helps magnify the things we want to pay attention to. At the same time, it eases our emotions and helps us to become peaceful. Therefore, make pondering during meditation a daily habit, and watch how significantly your emotions are soothed and solutions come to surface.

Oftentimes, we can't achieve the peaceful feelings we desire because of our environment and the negativity that surrounds us. During meditation, it is a good idea to perform a *negativity check*, which is a cleansing that helps detect the things that are keeping us from achieving ultimate peace.

While utilizing the negativity check technique, we clear our minds, honestly play back events that have occurred, and analyze the people and experiences we have encountered, as well as the places we have gone. Focus on each of these elements and honestly assess the things you need to change. When we go back in thought we are able to clearly see the people, places, and things that have been imposing on our peace. For example, your day can be going great until you get to work and come in contact with a certain co-worker, or you get a call from a certain so-called friend. It is important to do a negativity check to analyze the very points where our joy becomes interrupted. During meditation, we are able to see the picture more clearly. Instead of being inside the situation, we are able to see the situation from the outside.

A negativity check is a cleansing for our spirits. It helps us identify and then remove the people, places, and things that are hindering our quality of life.

It is common to be disrupted by other people's negativity. Energy is contagious! Do not allow anyone to put their trash in your can! Avoid negative people; they will only bring you down.

Have you ever been feeling good, and then you go around a particular person, who constantly tells you about all their troubles and misfortunes? Or, they always have something negative to say? Do you see how drained you become after you leave that person? That is the power of negative energy! It has the strength to zap your positive energy and bring you down! Therefore, avoid negative people like you would avoid the plague! Surround yourself with good people who have positive energy. Go places that make you feel happy and acquire things that bring you joy!

Growth and change are impossible without meditation. Nothing can be accomplished without your "Higher Power" and focused thought. Use this season to learn how to tap into the power of "self" through these various forms of meditation.

Is your growth and advancement important to you? If so, let's make a commitment together to take out time daily to meditate. Say this affirmation with me: "Today, I possess the power to change my course in life. I can do so in my secret closet of meditation. Each day before I start my day, I will meditate. I will see myself successfully accomplishing my tasks for the day. When times get rough and negative emotions approach, I will change my course by meditating. Any time I experience an event, or a feeling, I wish to change, I will stop and rid myself of negative thoughts through meditation. Before I close my eyes to sleep, I will meditate. I will replay the events of the day in my mind and fix those things I wish to change. Today, I am successful. I have the power to overcome. I will honor my new ability by constantly working to improve my skill set of meditation."

Congratulations! You have taken another huge step. It is now up to you to make meditation a habit. Remember, a habit is formed by disciplining yourself daily to perform the task you desire to master. You now have the power to sharpen this skillset, which will take you to levels you never imagined!

QUESTIONS

1. What is meditation?
2. Why is meditation important?
3. Name the four techniques of meditation we discussed in this chapter and how we utilize them?
4. What is visualization?
5. What is the acronym for fear?
6. Why can negative thoughts be deadly?
7. What is the key to enjoying a peaceful life?

WRITING ASSIGNMENT

Write out your own personal affirmation of goals you want to accomplish this month. Say your affirmation daily. Then meditate and ponder on your thoughts. Do this exercise daily and watch how smoothly and quickly you will accomplish your goals!

IV. LEARNING FROM THE PAST, THEN LETTING IT GO

POINT 4:

"If I hold on to shame and guilt, my spirit will always be low. So, I will learn from my past, acknowledge my mistakes, and then simply let them go."

As prisoner #59253-03, for many years I carried mountain loads of shame on my back. I couldn't help but repeat in my mind all the bad things the US Attorney in my case had to say about me. I constantly thought about the newspaper articles that were written about me and how I caused my family so much pain and humiliation. My parents were sued by my alleged victim – Lehman Brothers Bank, and they had to pay a $400,000 judgement from their pension to cover my incurred debt to the bank. On top of that, I left two small children behind to be raised by my family. Daily my mistakes blared in the innermost part of my soul with fierce conviction. In my mind, I was an ultimate failure. Stuck in that state I found it hard to move.

Even after I finally begin to forgive myself, I wanted to hide the past and bury it far from my memory. I hadn't realized at the time my story was actually my glory. It took many years to push past shame and guilt, but when I finally let it go, my life began to blossom.

It wasn't until my back was up against the wall that I was fueled into action. It was 2014 and I was on my last appeal efforts to the court. Prior to my sentencing my parents hired an appeals attorney. After giving him over $50,000 of their hard-earned pension funds, he ran off and never filed one single motion on my behalf. Consequently, I had to become my own attorney. I spent endless nights studying the law and finally found two major loopholes in my case.

Just fifty-nine days after I was sentenced, the bank I allegedly victimized collapsed. The very conduct they accused me of was exposed during the bank's bankruptcy findings. The newly discovered evidence that overwhelmingly supported my defense was now available and I finally had a shot at getting a new trial. Despite the good news, I had a fierce component in the bank's attorney. They had a high-powered team that seemed to have abundant connections within the courts.

After receiving a denial on my 2255 Motion for a New Trial and seeing my sentencing judge blatantly misinterpret the law in his denial of my motion, I decided it was finally time to tell my story. I stepped out on faith and created a book called "The High Price I Had to Pay." In this book, I detailed the events that led up to my arrest and the many injustices I encountered in the legal system, including receiving a six and a half year greater sentence than my white male co-defendants who instructed me on what to do.

Leaving no stone untold, I finally published my memoir. My strategy was to send it to every judge on the Third Circuit Court of Appeals where my final motion was being heard. My goal was to get the truth in front of the judges so their hearts would be turned in my favor. I never anticipated what happened next!

I can't tell you exactly what occurred in the courthouse when my book landed. I would have paid anything to have been a fly on the wall. Yet, I can tell you I received a furious letter from the Court of Appeals Clerk, stating I had no right to mail the book to all the judges. Mind you, the book stated names and revealed all the dirt I could substantiate that my prosecutors and team were involved in behind the scenes. It also connected the dots with articles written that supported my claims. I didn't know how potent my attempt to strike back was until the savvy bank lawyers finally backed down.

For years, multiple lawsuits piled up against me and my family, including the judgement that was issued against my parents. Every other week, I received stacks of legal documents in the mail that disturbed my soul with its contents. I read motion on top of motion that described me as what was made out to be the worst villain in the world. Suddenly, after I wrote the book, the court papers stopped.

Simultaneously, I used my legal skills to obtain a judgement against my former attorney who stole my money and never submitted one document on my behalf. I included the judgment order I won against him along with my books to the Court of Appeals. In my motion, I also shed light on my attorney's close connection to my prosecutors, which I was unaware of at the time I hired him. For sure I felt like I would finally get justice. However, I was not prepared for the way the scales started to balance.

The missile was launched and there was no turning back. Although I was scared inside because I didn't know what type of retaliation I would receive, at the same time, I felt liberated. While I waited patiently for the court's decision, my book skyrocketed on Amazon and I officially became a best-selling author from behind bars. More importantly to me, my colleagues, friends and family read the book and many of them had great compassion for me. Before the story was only told from the prosecutor's side, and although I admittedly accepted responsibility for my role, I certainly wasn't the culprit they portrayed as it was later proven that the bank itself invented the fraud that I was accused of master minding. My courage to speak out freed me internally.

Although I never received my freedom from the courts, I scored a different type of win. I was finally able to release the many layers of shame and guilt that kept me bound for so long. And, I knew it was only a matter of time that I would finally be physically free and use my experience as a stepping stool to a great future. So, I did in fact, win back my freedom. I learned from my past, acknowledged my mistakes and let my shame and guilt go. And it felt oh so good!

One of our biggest human errors is harboring our past errors. As we previously discussed, life is an obstacle course of tests and trials. We will not always pass every test the first time around. This does not mean we do not have another chance to succeed. Our failures are simply practice for our success! We are to analyze our dilemmas, see where we went wrong, acknowledge our faults, then simply let the past go!

If we do not have the correct perspective of the purpose of our trials, which are to teach us and help us grow, it is easy to fall into the rut of despair. Without the correct perspective, we begin to feel like losers, or inadequate. These feelings can paralyze us and keep us stuck in depression. We must not allow that to happen! We become victorious when we correctly view our obstacles, learn from them, and then let them go!

Many of us are stagnant in life because we hold on to the emotions of guilt, regret, and shame. In this chapter, we will learn to deal with these negative emotions, so we can discard them and victoriously move ahead. Harboring negative emotions is deadly! Not only does it kill your spirit, it will also rob you of your health.

It is common to unconsciously hold on to negative feelings. When we become overwhelmed with the pressures of life, our natural reaction is to suppress our emotions. In an attempt to avoid the reality of our pain or discomfort, many seek out such things as drugs, alcohol, or even people to consume our time. We do this so we don't have to acknowledge the truth of what is bothering us. This is very harmful and dangerous. Suppressing emotions does not provide an outlet for release, and whatever is bottled up inside will eventually burst. These explosions can end in deadly results such as suicide.

We must refuse to let this outcome become our portion! We can counteract and defend ourselves by learning how to adequately deal with shame, guilt, and regret. As you learn these techniques and allow them to become one with you, you will feel an amazing release!

First, let's analyze each of these negative emotions and their causes. Guilt, according to *Merriam Webster's Dictionary*, is the fact of having committed a specified or implied offense or crime. The emotion of guilt exists to allow us to recognize that we have done something wrong. If guilt arises and alerts us to our wrongdoings and we change our behavior, it has a positive effect. In that case, guilt is simply the sensor that lets us know our actions are unacceptable. Understanding this truth, we know guilt is intended to help us change our course. After we make our necessary corrections, we are to immediately let guilt go! If not, it will paralyze us by turning into shame.

According to *Merriam-Webster's Dictionary*, shame is a painful emotion caused by a sense of guilt, unworthiness, or disgrace, which causes great disappointment. When we harbor guilt, it turns into shame. Shame is very destructive. It is a painful emotion that causes us to feel unworthy. If we allow shame to take root within us, it causes serious depression, disabling us from moving forward. Shameful people want to hide, and they believe they are unworthy of experiencing a good life. They inflict themselves with pain by believing deep down inside they deserve to feel pain. There is nothing good that comes out of shame! If you do not disperse the negative energy that comes from shame, you will quickly self-destruct!

Merriam-Webster's Dictionary defines regret as: to feel sorry or disappointed about an event or situation. It is an expression of grief or disappointment. Feelings of regret come from something we did or failed to do. It is okay to allow yourself to feel regret, just as it is okay to allow yourself to feel the feelings attached with guilt. The problem comes when we hold on to these feelings and do not let them disperse. Regret should signal that we need to accept responsibility for what we did or did not do. Then, we should take action and do something to correct our behavior. We counteract regret through action! As we act, these feelings will have no choice but to subside.

It is impossible to be productive and reach your potential while holding on to shame, guilt, and regret. Many people are challenged by these emotions and become paralyzed because they are unconscious that they exist. We must educate ourselves to the detriment of each of these emotions, so we can quickly rid ourselves of them.

As we learned, harboring emotions of shame, guilt, and regret is deadly. They tear down our drive and our self-esteem, leaving us to believe we are less than worthy. If we don't feel good about ourselves, others will not feel good about us either. According to the law of attraction, we attract into our lives the expressions we put into the universe. Therefore, if we are full of low self-esteem and shame, we will attract people who will abuse us. This occurs because we have unconsciously sent a signal into the atmosphere that said, "I wish to be abused because I am unworthy." Understanding this truth, it is vital that we work on "self," rid ourselves of these deadly feelings, and replace them with feelings of esteem and self-worth. Through this journey we will learn how to get rid of these negative emotions and fill ourselves up with positive energy!

Remember, life is all about learning. We would never learn if we did not experience obstacles. Therefore, we must embrace our obstacles by allowing ourselves to see them as opportunities to grow. No one on this earth is perfect; we all make mistakes and fall short of God's glory. Yet, it is essential not to get caught up in the mistake. Instead, get caught up in what you can do about it!

Life is not about how you fall; it is about how you get up. Just as a child who learns to walk falls before they are successful at walking, we will also fall at times. But we don't have to stay down! The key to overcoming life's hurdles is learning how to wipe off the defilements of life and keep on moving! Never allow yourself to stay stagnant because of your past mistakes! You cannot reverse time. The only thing you can do is make your future better by not making the same mistakes again. Therefore, you must deal with your past head on. Learn from your experience, and then simply let it go! It may be easier said than done. But when you master this technique, you will ultimately master life!

We learned in our previous lessons that God allows trials to occur to help us grow. When trials are sent to lead us into repentance, God allows us to feel the emotion of guilt to convict our hearts. Then, guilt is used to signal us to change our ways. It is not God's intention for us to stay stuck in guilt. He wants us to deal with our emotions by changing our actions, then discard our guilt.

Also, we previously discussed that we all have an enemy of our soul. The enemy purposely sends attacks to prevent us from achieving our purpose here on earth. Fear and shame are two of the biggest weapons the enemy uses to stunt our growth. He knows if we accept these emotions and harbor them, then we will eventually self-destruct.

The enemy works by replaying our mishaps or mistakes over and over through the thoughts he sends us. We may not even be thinking about an event, yet he continuously brings it up in our thoughts. Have you ever done something you knew you shouldn't have done and became remorseful? You repented of your sins, yet you still were constantly bombarded with shameful thoughts about what you did. That is the enemy at work! In order to win and receive the reward God has for you, you must reject these thoughts of shame. Refuse to allow the enemy to keep you bound!

To have a relationship with God is to know He is merciful. God doesn't want us to do bad things, but He understands that we are humans. All humans make mistakes! When we realize we have done wrong, God allows us the provision to repent and accept responsibility for our wrongdoings. When we are truly remorseful and take action to change our ways, God is ready to forgive us. All we have to simply do is ask Him for forgiveness. He forgives us and remembers our sins no more!

Sometimes it is common nature to blame someone else for our mistakes. I did that in the past all too well. Many times, I played the victim, so I wouldn't have to face the truth. One of the hardest things to deal with in my court case was not accepting responsibility for my own actions. In my mind, since the bankers were down with the scheme, what I was doing was okay. My intent was to get the loans and pay them back. So, I used that to justify my actions. I also harbored on the fact that the white, middle-aged mortgage broker and lawyer in my case both got two-year sentences each, while my sentence was more than six times greater than theirs. Yes, that was unfair. However, it didn't negate the fact that I chose to participate in a scheme that was illegal. I had to accept the fact that I was wrong. No one put a gun to my head. I choose to tread in a gray, and it ultimately led to my incarceration. The crazy thing is, when I finally accepted responsibility and took myself out of the mindset of being a victim, I was internally freed.

When we blame others, we only deceive ourselves. Instead of developing and maturing, our deceit leads us to remain stagnant by not changing our behavior patterns. To be truly successful in life, we must be honest with ourselves and others. Instead of hiding and covering up our mistakes, we must expose them. Acknowledging our faults is a sign of maturity. Only mature people are able to admit when they have done something wrong. The first step to maturity means honestly evaluating "self." We evaluate "self" in meditation, asking our "Higher Power" to show us where we have gone wrong and to expose our flaws.

When problems and situations arise, instead of getting angry, take a time out. Honestly ask yourself the question: "Have I played a role in causing this obstacle?" Especially when we run into problems with others, we must consider our own faults. That person may have issues, and he or she may not be nice, but did you say or do something that provoked that person's response? Honestly asking yourself these types of questions is part of properly analyzing your situation.

Analyzing and identifying our mistakes open the door for change and deliverance. Change is impossible if we refuse to acknowledge the need to fix our behavior. For instance, a parent may want their child to do the right things. The truth is, the child will not change until he or she has a desire to do so. This desire will not come until the child recognizes his or her own faults. With that in mind, trials are sent by God to help us see and acknowledge that we need to change and improve ourselves. When we hit rock bottom in life, we tend to accept that we need to do things differently.

After we honestly analyze our situation, we must be able to specifically identify where we went wrong so we can make the necessary adjustments. Acknowledging our faults can be very difficult and painful at times. Nobody wants to be wrong. It takes a mature person to recognize and admit their faults.

For example, Mary has a sister named Carol whom she greatly loves. Mary is a successful RN (registered nurse). She owns her own house and does very well for herself. Carol is not as fortunate and doesn't have the same ambition and drive as her sister, Mary. Carol gets jobs and starts off well, but eventually quits or gets fired when she becomes bored with her job. Mary knows her sister's problem, but she loves her despite her shortcomings.

One day, Mary talks to Carol and tries to convince her to go back to school, so she can get a better job. At first, Carol disagrees, but she tells Mary that she will go back to school if Mary becomes a co-signer on her new car purchase. Eager to see her sister achieve a degree, Mary decides to co-sign for Carol's new vehicle. Carol gets the car and enrolls in school. However, before the semester is over, Carol quits both school and her new job and is no longer able to pay her car note. Mary becomes very upset, as she is unable to afford Carol's extra bills.

Mary goes to Carol's house and they end up getting into a physical altercation. Anger quickly builds after Mary attempts to refinance her house and is turned down. Her bad credit rating is due to Carol's delinquent car payments. As a result of the altercation, Carol calls the police and Mary is arrested for assault and battery. After staying in jail for over a month, Mary loses her job as a nurse. Now Mary is jobless, and her house is in foreclosure. She is very depressed and believes Carol is the reason her whole world is turned upside down.

Just like many of us, Mary is experiencing a major obstacle. She has a choice. Either she can stay stagnant or take action.

The first thing Mary must do is analyze her situation. She has to play back the events from the beginning in her mind. When she does, she will recognize life was fine until she decided to sign for Carol's car. Her analyzation will lead her to discover she made a mistake when she willfully decided to be a guarantor for Carol.

The analysis is the easy part. We often can clearly see where we made our mistakes. The harder part is to admit and acknowledge our own faults. Mary wants to blame Carol, but the truth is Carol did not force Mary to get involved. Mary made her own decision to co-sign. Her love for Carol influenced her, but it is not Carol's fault. Mary should have been wise enough to observe her sister's past behavior and take that into account *before* she made the decision to co-sign. If Mary had learned to protect "self," she would have never put herself at risk.

For Mary to move forward, she must admit her fault of co-signing for Carol's car, after she already knew Carol's work ethic and character. She also has to admit her fault for getting angry and going to Carol's house with intentions to fight. When Mary acknowledges her role in the situation, she opens the door to healing and recovery.

After we acknowledge our faults, the next step is to take responsibility for our actions. Taking responsibility is not just saying, "I'm wrong." It is to do something to prevent us from making the same mistakes again. Taking responsibility is essentially improving "self." It is analyzing our areas of weakness and doing something about them.

When mature people do something wrong, they admit their faults, which can include apologizing to the party whom they hurt and attempting to fix the situation. Taking responsibility is an active choice. It is not fumbling around feeling sorry for yourself. It is getting up and doing something to ensure this situation will never arise again.

Mary decided to get up one day and go to church. She listened to the minister talk about forgiveness and starting out on a brand-new slate. That day Mary decided to make amends with her sister and acknowledged her own fault for co-signing for Carol's car. Mary greatly missed her sister, as the two of them hadn't spoken in several months. In an attempt to make matters right, Mary decided to send Carol a bouquet of flowers. On the card she wrote:

I miss you and I love you, no matter what we go through.
Love Mary.

When Carol received the bouquet of flowers she cried. Mary's actions sparked a change in Carol's life.

Carol realized her faults and decided to accept responsibility for her actions. too. She went to a friend to discuss what she could do to fix the problem. Carol's friend led her to the Judge that sentenced Mary. Carol told the Judge the whole story. He was touched by Mary's attempt to reconcile her relationship with her sister, so he reversed Mary's conviction. Then, Carol called the finance company and worked out a new repayment plan. Determined to keep up with the agreement, Carol got a good job and enrolled back into school.

Sometime later, Carol went to Mary's new home, a small apartment in a run down area, and informed Mary about all the steps she had taken. The sisters reconciled and cried in each other's arms. Mary ended up getting her job back and saved her house, and Carol ended up becoming a successful schoolteacher, who loves her job.

There is a lot we can learn from Mary and Carol on both sides. No matter how bad our situations seem, there is always a solution. If we are willing to do the work, we will find it. All solutions come by working on "self." As we mature in our spiritual walk, we learn to improve "self." As we improve "self," we essentially improve the quality of our lives. As we change, our circumstances begin to change, too. The things that used to bother us will not bother us anymore. In addition, when we change "self," it will cause people to act differently toward us. That is, because we become wise in choosing our actions, which makes others react differently. Life takes on a new meaning when we tap into the power of "self!"

In the last section of this chapter, we will discuss the detrimental consequences of un-forgiveness. To get over our obstacles, we must open our hearts to forgive. If not, we will always stay handcuffed to our past!

Just like Mary, many of us have been hurt by people we love in our past. In fact, it is hard to be hurt by people you don't love, unless someone physically hurts you. Many of us have held onto this pain, which eventually turned into bitterness or hate. When we hate others and refuse to forgive them, God will not forgive us! As a result, we block our blessings from our "Higher Power."

Forgiving others is not for those who have wronged us; it is for us! It takes a lot of energy to harbor hate. As we hold on to feelings of bitterness and hate, through the law of attraction we send a signal into the universe that sends bitterness and hate back to us. We also handcuff ourselves to our past through the offense and remain bound to our feelings of unforgiveness, which stunts healing and mobility.

People do bad things when they accept negative thoughts from the enemy of their souls. Just as the enemy sends us negative thoughts of fear, shame, and guilt, he also puts bad thoughts into people's minds, influencing them to do the wrong things. The enemy's desire is to control that person, so he can inflict harm to others by using them. As a result, the person becomes a pawn for the enemy and doesn't even know it! They have no control over their lives because they haven't learned how to take control of their minds. Just as you are a victim of that person, that person is a victim of the enemy. Their lives will ultimately self-destruct until they change their hearts and their mindsets.

When we stay locked in unforgiveness, we allow the negative cycle to continue. That is the enemy's plan. He knows he can keep us from achieving God's purpose, if he keeps us out of the will of God. Don't let the enemy win in his wicked plot! Break the enemy's chains by forgiving yourself and others who have harmed you in the past.

Forgiveness is a personal act done with you and your "Higher Power." It is an act of cleansing your heart of ill feelings toward yourself for your mistakes, and toward others for their actions toward you. Forgiveness doesn't mean you have to tell the person who harmed you "I forgive you;" that is a personal choice that takes courage and time. Forgiveness is simply cleansing your mind of the defilement done and praying to your "Higher Power" to open that person's eyes to see their faults so they can change.

We are to leave all vengeance in God's hands. Never try to get someone back for the wrong they have committed; it will only cause you more hurt and harm! Leave their punishment up to God. His wrath is perfect, and it causes change!

Forgiving frees our conscience and puts us at peace with ourselves and others. We no longer allow our minds to ponder on our mistakes or the mistakes of others. Instead we become focused on having a prosperous future.

Forgiving yourself is essential to your success. It is the act of getting rid of all shame and guilt. It is saying to yourself, "I've made some mistakes, but it is okay. I learned from them and these experiences will make me stronger, wiser, and better."

As we forgive, we drop all the heavy weights off our shoulders. We give ourselves permission to move on by allowing "self" to feel worthy to achieve again. Forgiveness generates the positive energy we need to propel us ahead in life. Without forgiveness we cannot change for the better!

Are you ready to move forward in life and break loose from the chains that have you bound? If so, follow me in this prayer: "God, I come to You today with an offering of thanksgiving. I am grateful that You have exposed the areas in my life that I need to work on. I ask You to continue to reveal my shortcomings, so I can improve them. I ask You for assistance in helping me analyze my mistakes, acknowledge my faults, and accept responsibility for my actions. Help me rid myself of shame, guilt, regret, and un-forgiveness. Give me supernatural wisdom and knowledge on what I need to do to keep these feelings out of my life permanently.

"Now I ask You to forgive me of all of my sins and help me to forgive myself and all others who have hurt me. Cleanse my spirit and give me a clean heart to love again. I now thank You for magnificent results, as I stand today in expectancy of Your mighty move on my behalf! Cover me and protect me from evil and open my eyes to receive understanding. Amen."

Congratulations! You have made another huge step. So many people stay in darkness and inflict self-pain because they are unable to heal from their past. Today, you have opened the doors to your healing process. Don't stop, continue to move forward diligently. You are destined for success!

QUESTIONS

1. What is shame, guilt, and regret?
2. How can harboring these feelings be dangerous to you?
3. What are the steps to rid yourself of shame, guilt, and regret?
4. What is un-forgiveness?
5. Why is un-forgiveness dangerous?
6. What is the enemy's purpose for shame and un-forgiveness?
7. What is God's purpose for guilt?

WRITING ASSIGNMENT

Analyze your current dilemma and write out your faults. Describe some ways you can prevent yourself from making the same mistakes again. Write out an acclamation of what you will do to keep yourself from falling into the traps of shame, guilt, regret, and un-forgiveness in the future.

V. FIGURING OUT WHAT YOU CAN DO

POINT 5:

"When life seems hopeless, I must change my point of view. That's how I regroup to figure out what I can do."

It is common to feel hopeless when we encounter unexpected obstacles. When we don't have control over what is going on, our hopelessness can lead to despair, which often turns into depression. In this state, we lose the willpower to push forward and become stuck.

The only way to get over a hurdle is to work our way through it! Obstacles are sent to challenge our growth. Becoming lazy during a trial can be destructive. The longer we do nothing about our problems, the more chaos it will create in other areas of our lives, sometimes doubling or even quadrupling the dilemma. Therefore, the best thing to do when an obstacle arises is to deal with it! Here

are the four steps to facing your barriers head on:
1. Now that we have our "Higher Power" as our Partner, we should seek God first for divine wisdom and knowledge.
2. Wait on God to give us the answers we need to be placed on the correct path.
3. Analyze our situation in meditation, so we can determine our error(s) and where we may need to change our course.
4. Figure out what we can do to overcome our dilemma.

It is important that we do not skip steps in our process of deliverance. Many people understand the need to seek their "Higher Power" for help. Yet, they miss the second part. God is our Partner, meaning we must work in unison with Him. When we do our part, He will do His! It is good to have faith in God, but faith without work behind it is dead!

In this chapter, we will study how to evaluate our options and figure out what we can do to overcome our dilemmas. Doing our part secures our success. Remember, during your challenge, this obstacle was sent to advance you and make you grow! You advance when you expand your abilities, as well as your intellect. This occurs by taking the initiative to work on and develop "self." You cannot expect your "Higher Power" to do all the work for you. It is now time to pull up your sleeves and embrace this opportunity to grow. Growth comes from within. This is the season to work on and develop "self." As you grow, what once appeared to be a challenge will no longer faze you, because you have gained the wisdom and knowledge to overcome!

After you finish the assignments in the previous chapters and complete your meditation, it is time to get to work! Pull out your journal and start writing your analysis of your current situation. Your analysis starts out by first identifying your problem. Be sure to answer these questions:

- Why do you believe it came about?
- Did you have any fault in creating the situation?
- What good can come out of this situation?
- What lessons can you learn?
- What steps can you take in the future to not repeat this same dilemma?
- What is your desired outcome?

When you answer these questions, be specific and provide details. This will form the road map you need to help you out of your rut and stay out of it permanently. It is vital that you take the time to process your answers accurately.

After you have written down your complete analyzation, it is time to intently examine your findings and determine what you can do to take an active part in achieving your desired outcome. Use a separate sheet of paper and entitle it, "My Conclusion Report." From the answers you provided, write out what you can do to overcome your obstacle in detailed steps. The conclusion should then be written as an affirmation. For example: "Today, I have discovered the solution to my problem. My obstacle is no longer an obstacle; it is now my opportunity to advance. I will grow by (In great detail, list the steps you will take to overcome your obstacle):

This conclusion report should be kept with you at all times. It should be read in the morning along with your daily meditations. When you have free time during the day, it should also be read again. In addition, it should also be read at night, so you can meditate on the steps you must take prior to going to sleep.

As you travel through your journey and find new discoveries of things you need to do, add them to your list. Also, as you complete each step, cross it off your list. The more steps you complete and cross off your list, the better you will begin to feel about yourself. This displays your growth!

When we can see our growth, it inspires and encourages us to push ourselves to greater levels. Our work then increases our faith, which causes our "Higher Power" to get involved in helping us achieve our goals. If this step is properly followed, the results will be amazing!

It is important to understand that all growth comes with work, which requires discipline. Becoming an overcomer also requires persistence! You cannot do the work one day and then stop, still expecting positive results. You must be determined to follow your mission through until completion! That is the only way you will be able to see the fruits of your labor.

As we advance to new levels in our lives, our obstacles become more challenging. There will be times when we don't have the solutions to our problems, and we have no clue what to do. In the next section of this chapter, we will discuss options to get clarity on what we can do.

If you are going through a problem that is difficult to solve, you must first seek your "Higher Power." Ask Him to give you clarity and send you the provisions you need to overcome your obstacles. Also ask Him to guide you to the right people, places, and things that can assist you on your journey. After you have completed the task of going to your "Higher Power," it is time to roll up your sleeves and seek the provisions you have requested in your prayer. This is the step where most people get confused. They believe when there is nothing they know how to physically do, and they go to God for His help, that concludes their work. This is incorrect! They have successfully completed the first step by seeking guidance. Yet, they have neglected to seek out the provisions they requested by doing their own due diligence.

In the Bible, Matthew 7:7-8 says:

"*Ask*, and it will be given to you; *seek* and you will find; *knock*, and it will be opened. For everyone who asks receives, and he who seeks finds, and to him who knocks it will be opened."

Notice in this verse the words *ask*, *seek*, and *knock* are used. It doesn't just say, "Ask, and it will be given to you!" That is because our Creator desires us to do some work. The work we must do will help us to develop and grow. As we work and seek, we will find the answers. As we knock on doors searching for the answers, doors will be opened for us. Knowing this truth, it's time to do something about our problems! We have more power than we think!

There is nothing new under the sun. Anything that is happening now has happened before. Even if it seems as if no one is going through the things you are encountering, that is not true. You are not alone in your struggles. Someone else has already gone through what you are experiencing, and someone else has already overcome! Therefore, it is our job to research and seek the knowledge they used to succeed.

After you complete your evaluation, talk about your issues with trusted friends and family. Many success stories are created in the company of wise counsel. By discussing your issues, you can gain wisdom from others who may have already experienced what you have gone through. If your friends or family members can't help you, they may lead you to someone else who can. By opening your mouth and talking about your issues, you can be led to the correct source for help.

Furthermore, you also have the option of seeking professional help. Professionals spend many years learning their trade. They have advanced wisdom and knowledge in their area of expertise. God sends us professionals to help us in our dilemmas. It is up to us to take advantage of their services.

You can find good professional services through word of mouth. You can also go online and research top professionals in the field of your need. Seek out others who have used their services and were pleased. Seeking the help of professional services can save you a lot of time and a lot of headaches. You cannot expect to know what someone has learned over many years in a short period of time. Through their course of trial and error and schooling, they have learned how to avoid mistakes and mishaps. Therefore, it is a wise thing to seek the assistance of a good professional in your area of need! They will help you expand your knowledge and lead you in the direction of solution.

Another way to receive help is to read books that address your problems. There are millions of books that have been written on your current issue, which are at your disposal. Remember, you are not the only one who has ever experienced your problems! Therefore, go to your local library or bookstore and research the books written on your topic of need. You can also research these books on the internet by putting your subject into the search engine, followed by the word "books." You'll be surprised what information is available to you in books. Someone who has gone through your same dilemmas has written a blueprint for you to follow. The key to your recovery is knowledge. Many people fail in life because of a lack of knowledge. Don't fail! Make it your goal to receive as much knowledge as you can in your areas of concern, and you indeed will become an overcomer!

Research is vital when you are trying to prevail over complex issues. We live in a computer age where vast amounts of information are available to us by simply accessing the web. You can gain tons of knowledge by spending time doing research at home. The more you become informed, the easier it will be to access the information you need, which will lead to your solution. Research requires diligence. One piece of information may lead you to several other sources of information. Therefore, be determined to patiently go through the material you discover. Set out a specific amount of time each day to seek the knowledge you wish to obtain. Your persistence and dedication will lead you into your desired results!

As you begin to read books on your topic of need, you will find out how inspiring reading can be! You will learn that you are not alone in the world with your dilemmas. The stories of other overcomers will inspire you to push ahead. Words are containers of power. As you read, your faith will strengthen, giving you the energy to leap over your hurdle!

During your research period, don't neglect referring to your Holy Book. Find out first what your Holy Book says about the subject matter. When we are feeling low and need a boost in our spirits, one of the greatest resources we can use is turning to our Holy Book. Never neglect the wisdom and knowledge available to you in your Holy Book. If you are unsure of which passage to read in the Holy Book, refer to the table of contents or concordance. You can also ask your spiritual advisors which passages you should read. Study the passages and verses that apply to you and use these passages in your daily meditation.

Our Holy Books are filled with stories of overcomers. These awesome passages lift our faith when we see how God brought His children through. We know our "Higher Power" is no respecter of persons. What He did for others in ancient times, He can do the same for us today!

In this last section I will outline some specific examples and available options for seeking help. This will illuminate pathways to different outlets of guidance.

EXAMPLE 1

The knowledge that you have obtained in this book came about as a result of my imprisonment. As I mentioned in the introduction of this book, I became a multi-millionaire by the age of 25. I was very ambitious, yet my ambition led to compromise, which ultimately led to my incarceration. Due to the amount of money involved in my crime, I was sentenced (at the age of 31) to twelve and a half years in Federal Prison. I never expected this lengthy sentence and to me, my life as I knew it was over! I went from a plush, luxurious lifestyle, to sharing a bunk bed in a 5½ x 9 jail cell. I desperately wanted to close my eyes and just die! I often watched the television and saw my successful peers soar, while I lay captive in my prison cell. Many nights I cried out to God seeking the solution to my dilemma.

During my imprisonment I began to spend many hours reading my Bible and other self-help books that helped me re-evaluate my life. I learned I was actually living in spiritual prison many years before I was actually incarcerated. Prison gave me the reality check I needed to examine "self." As I began to work on "self," I was able to tap into the knowledge that is enclosed within this book.

After I analyzed myself, I knew it was time to do something about my situation. My research led me to a source who was familiar with Federal law and agreed to work on helping me reverse my conviction.

While I awaited my release, I considered how I could help others around me. My imprisonment opened my heart to the concerns of other incarcerated women. I utilized my time to create the Voices of Consequence Enrichment Series, a series of self-help books that promote the rehabilitation of incarcerated women. As I saw the effectiveness of my books amongst the inmate population, it increased my faith to write self-help books for the general public. As a result, you now hold this self-help book in your hands!

Alone in a lonely cell, I discovered my talent for writing, which was not my previous profession. Through writing, I gained a sense of fulfillment I never experienced when I was free. I created a partnership with my "Higher Power" and allowed him to use me to help others who also faced trials and tribulations.

Initially, imprisonment seemed like the worst thing that could ever happen, but for me it became my rescue ship for change! It was the time I needed away from the world that changed my perspective on how I viewed life.

EXAMPLE 2

Dorothy and John were high school sweethearts who married at an early age. Both Dorothy and John worked hard, saved their money, and desperately wanted to start a family. For many years Dorothy tried to have a son, yet she was unable to carry a baby full term. Dorothy sought the help of a physician, and she was finally able to have a baby boy whom she named Chris.

From the day of his birth, Chris was spoiled. Dorothy detached from all her previous obligations in order to raise her son the right way. She enrolled him (at a young age) in every extra-curricular activity she could think of. Chris played basketball, football, baseball, and karate. He was also a Boy Scout and involved in multiple after-school activities.

Dorothy lived life through Chris. His mere presence gave her inner strength. Life for Dorothy and John was all about Chris!

As Chris grew older, he started hanging out with the wrong crowd. Chris had Dorothy wrapped around his finger and would often manipulate her and deceive her regarding his actual whereabouts. Right before Dorothy's eyes, Chris began to change, and Dorothy couldn't understand why? Even still, she loved him unconditionally. Chris began to abuse heroin, but neither John nor Dorothy were aware of what he was doing, even though they saw a huge change in his behavior. They thought very highly of their son and wouldn't ever believe he would become a drug addict.

One night while hanging out with friends, Chris overdosed on heroin and he died in the bathroom of his best friend's house.

John and Dorothy were alerted to their son's unexpected death, and they were both devastated! Dorothy went into severe depression and even had to be checked into a mental institution after having a nervous breakdown.

At the mental hospital, Dorothy got a visit from a lady who helped her find her "Higher Power," and as a result, Dorothy began to recover. She had a deep desire to discover the meaning behind her misfortune. During her time of meditation, Dorothy was led into revelations about her shortcomings and discovered her purpose.

Dorothy healed from losing her only son, Chris, by creating a foundation that helps addicted teens and their parents. Dorothy named the foundation after Chris. To date, Dorothy's foundation and Chris's story has helped ti inspire hundreds of teens to abstain from drugs or get the help they needed to get off of them. Today Dorothy hears numerous testimonies about the assistance her foundation supplies, which brings her great joy. Each story helps her keep Chris's legacy alive in her memory.

A couple of years after forming the foundation, Dorothy discovered she was pregnant again. She now has a beautiful little girl name Crystal. The family is happy and prosperous, and Chris's legacy will forever live on!

EXAMPLE 3

Betty worked hard at her job as a secretary for over fifteen years. She was loyal and very dedicated to her boss. Betty had a great talent for baking and would often bring in treats for her co-workers, including her boss. As time went by, Betty's boss ended up retiring and a younger man came in as his replacement. Betty was very essential in helping her new boss obtain order in his new position. He learned a lot from Betty as she had great organizational and leadership skills.

After a year, he got the nuggets he needed from Betty and became successful. Shortly after, Betty's married boss began to have an affair with a young receptionist in the company. Betty couldn't help but observe the overly friendly behavior that occurred between her boss and the receptionist. Although she took offense to the activities, especially because she liked the boss's wife, Betty dared not say a word. Betty's boss took notice of her change of behavior. Afraid Betty would alert his wife, he decided to get rid of Betty and replace her with an inexperienced employee.

After fifteen years of dedication and service, one day Betty came to work and was told her services were no longer needed. Devastated, Betty went into a deep depression. While watching an inspirational television show, Betty got the courage to begin again and seek her "Higher Power" for direction. Betty's savings were almost depleted, and she no longer had a source of income. She spent many months searching for a job, but her age made her a target of discrimination.

One day while in the grocery store, Betty bumped into one of her old co-workers who was so happy to see her. She told Betty the company was in shambles and the boss had fired her replacement because she was incompetent and caused several mishaps at the job. The woman told Betty she was getting married, and Betty offered to make the woman's wedding cake.

Even under financial distress, Betty donated her services to her co-worker and made a fabulous cake that everybody who attended the wedding talked about! Afterward, Betty got several orders and decided to start a bakery out of her kitchen. Betty's bakery took off, and she began to make more money than she could ever dream about making, much more than she received at her previous job.

As time passed, Betty's first boss called her upon hearing that she had been fired. He was extremely angry because he knew how loyal and dedicated Betty was. He asked if she had gotten the money from the retirement account he had set up for her when she was first employed. Betty was unaware of this money, but her first boss helped her redeem it. When she received the large lump sum check in the mail, Betty was overwhelmed.

Immediately, she opened a new bank account and put some of the money in savings and the rest she used to open up her own bakery.

Today, Betty's bakery is a franchise. Millions of people enjoy her fabulous recipes! What Betty thought was her worst misfortune turned out to be her greatest opportunity for advancement!

EXAMPLE 4

Gary and Jessica met in college and fell in love. Jessica got pregnant so the two decided to get married, and Gary quit school so he could take on a full-time job. The couple was doing well at first, but the burdens of their finances often caused bickering between the two.

While Jessica stayed home with the baby and completed school, Gary picked up a second job. Things got better as the second income helped sustain them.

Eventually, Jessica completed school and became a successful nurse. She made more money than Gary because of her skill set and her college degree. Her greater income led her to be prideful, as she now carried most of the weight for their expenses.

Gary started to feel like less of a man and was degraded by Jessica's insults. He went into a deep depression when he found out his wife might be having dealings with one of the doctors at the hospital. Gary withdrew from his wife, quit his job, and went back home to live with his parents.

One day Gary's mother was able to convince him to come with her to worship service. Weak from his dilemma, bit by bit Gary gained strength and faith at the house of worship. One of the members gave him Rick Warren's, *Purpose Driven Life*, and Gary began to utilize the steps in the book. He decided it was time to find his purpose.

Thereafter, Gary went back to work and took on a job that allowed him to go back to school. He reached out to his wife and began to help out with the family's bills. Gary worked at a pet shop and discovered his passion was working with animals. He enrolled in school and received his degree in veterinary science and became a successful veterinarian.

During Gary's and Jessica's separation, Jessica began to appreciate and love Gary more. She realized how he selflessly quit school and worked two jobs, which enabled her to stay in school. Also, she saw his deep care and compassion for their daughter. The two ended up going to marriage counseling and agreed to reconcile.

Today, Gary and Jessica have two more beautiful children, and they are both living a joyous life, doing the things which make them both happy. Their hardships have helped them to appreciate each other more, and they've tightened their marital bond.

I shared these stories with you to remind you that your obstacle doesn't have to be your end! You can get through this thing. You can make it! It's important that you take this time to evaluate your shortcomings and work on "self." As you change, the situations around you will ultimately change too! The solution for our troubles lies within. It's up to you to take out the time to discover it.

Are you ready to roll up your sleeves? Are you tired of sitting around waiting for the storm to pass? Well, get up and let's do something about it! If you are ready to work on your problems, say this acclamation with me:

"Today, I will no longer sit back and do nothing! I will get up and do everything I can to change my current circumstances. I know I am not alone. I have the help and assistance of my Partner, which is my "Higher Power." Daily, I will review my situations and figure out what I can do to turn them around. If I don't have the answers, I will seek for them. If I seek and still don't find them, I will knock on the door of help and assistance from others. Whatever I do I will not remain stagnant. I will search until I find the wisdom and knowledge I need to overcome this hurdle. I will not give up! I am an overcomer! I will survive! I will look this giant of an obstacle in the face, and I will command it to move! I will beat it down with my faith and persistence until it no longer exists! This situation will not kill me, instead it will make me strong! I am built to outlast this storm!"

Write this affirmation down and put it in your wallet. When times get rough, read it and remind yourself to take the steps you need to actively overcome.

Congratulations! You have taken another huge step. You have equipped yourself with the information you need to get busy working on overcoming your obstacle. Read this chapter again. Study the points and allow them to become one with you.

QUESTIONS

1. What are some questions that you need to answer in your written analysis of your situation?
2. What information do you include in your conclusion report?
3. If you don't have the solution to your problems, what sources can you go to for help?
4. What does it mean to Ask, Seek, and Knock for your solution?
5. Why is it good to talk about your problems with others you trust?
6. How can reading be helpful in finding your solution?
7. How can an obstacle turn into your greatest opportunity to succeed?

WRITING ASSIGNMENT

Complete your problem analysis and your conclusion report in your journal and keep them within arm's reach.

VI. LEARNING TO CARE FOR "SELF"

POINT 6:

"I am my greatest asset, the temple that holds my wealth. So, I must make me a priority, and always care for "self."

We live in a society where self-hate is rampant. Everyday people are constantly inflicting self-pain and allowing others to abuse them because they feel unworthy. Society has brainwashed us with its so-called standards of success. We constantly look at television, the newspapers, and magazines, viewing what others deems as successful. We then develop the desire to look a certain way, wear a certain type of clothes, drive a certain type of car, marry a certain type of person and have a certain kind of career, all to keep up with the Joneses! Only to figure out in the end that the Joneses don't even live on our block! It was all an illusion.

Things aren't always what they seem! Remember, the enemy sends us illusions of **f**alse **e**vidence that **a**ppears **r**eal. We see people's lives from the outside, but we often don't get to see the inside. Many of us are chasing people, places, and things which we believe will create our ultimate satisfaction, and those things we are chasing, in essence, have no real value! It's like a big beautiful box ornately wrapped but has nothing in it! Take a closer look at how many wealthy people and celebrities flood the news with their constant problems. We view them as successful, but what is success without true happiness? Remember, a person's happiness will never come from external things, or people. True happiness is only derived from within. Happiness occurs by tapping into "self."

I had millions of dollars, several mansions on top of the hills and enough cars to ride a new one every day of the week, however, inside I was empty and void. I had used material things to hide the real pain I was dealing inside. The pain of not feeling good enough and really being insecure, but telling another story to the world I encountered. I chased after the esteem and affection of others to make me happy, making people, places and things my idol and they all turned on me. It wasn't until that happened that I began to face my own demons. I didn't even know what I liked or what made me happy, because I was so reliant on the feelings of others. While incarcerated I realized I failed to care for myself properly and that lack caused me so much harm.

In this chapter we will discuss the importance of self-care. We will learn the key to maintaining our joy, no matter what circumstances and situations we endure. Essentially, this chapter will give you the fundamentals to increase your value and expand your self-worth.

Many of us have gotten so caught up with chasing fulfillment through people, places, and things that we have neglected "self." Many of our goals and dreams have been based on the likes and desires of others, and not ourselves. We have lived life to please people and make them happy. Basically, our happiness has been based on our ability to make others happy. Many of us have been so swept away by this way of life, that we have lost our true identity. Consequently, storms have arisen in our lives, purposed by God, and we are now left in constant confusion and disarray.

For some of us, God has purposely separated us from our idols, or the people we worked so hard to please, leaving us faced with the reality that we have done very little to care for "self." Our whole life has been based on catering to someone else's needs. We look at ourselves and feel hopeless, not knowing what to do because we are so used to caring for another person, and we thrived off the false esteem from doing so. We felt as though our self-worth came from gaining the attention and love of someone else. Instead of realizing our error and working on self, we desperately sought after new people to repeat the cycle with. We begin a new relationship, only to find out this relationship does not work either! We sob and wallow in despair, not understanding why our relationships don't seem to work out, missing the mark or the purpose of our obstacles.

Fulfillment in life will never come from a relationship with a person! Fulfillment comes from developing a relationship with your "Higher Power" and tapping into your purpose! Until you take the necessary steps to work on "self," which will lead you to purpose, you will remain broken inside. Wholeness comes when you tap into the power of "self."

When two broken people come together in a relationship, there will always be constant chaos and confusion. Each party expects the other to satisfy "self" and make them whole. Both individuals are looking for the other to do for them what only God can do when we spend time improving "self." In this case, two halves don't make a whole; it creates a catastrophe! God will never allow your idol (anyone or anything you put before Him) to satisfy you! He will purposely send an obstacle your way to illuminate your flaws! You will remain in the same position until you readjust your priorities.

You can't expect to be an asset to any relationship until you are emotionally whole yourself. When you discover "self," you then have the ability to share your secret of success with your significant other. Wholeness comes when you work in union with your "Higher Power" to discover your purpose. You no longer remain needy, suffocating your partner by looking for excessive time, attention, and fulfillment. You learn how to give yourself the time and attention you need to maintain your inner joy. What others neglect to do for you, you begin to do for yourself. Your life is no longer governed by the other person and their actions. Your life becomes purposed centered. If they are there and they contribute to your quality of life, great! If not, and they decide to separate from you, that's okay too! Either way, you are content because you look to your source, which is your "Higher Power," and no longer to man. You no longer become afraid of being alone because you now have the assurance that you are never alone. Your Partner, which is your "Higher Power," always has your back and your best interest at heart!

When we come to the conclusion that we no longer want to be people pleasers, and we want to become God pleasers instead, we have to pull up our sleeves and do some work. We have to go back to the basics and learn to discover "self."

Discovering "self" comes when we take out time to meditate and focus on what brings us inner joy. Each of us were uniquely designed by God. We were each created specifically with our purpose in mind. God has given each of us inner desires. When we follow our God-given desires, we ultimately tap into purpose.

During meditation we must spend time getting to know what we truly like. The first thing to ask yourself during meditation is: "What do I enjoy doing?" Spend time clearly analyzing the things you do that bring you joy. What do you do effortlessly that others admire? When you take time to focus on these things, you are able to tap into your God-given skills and talents.

The next question to ask yourself is: "What do I do that makes me feel good about myself?" When you honestly analyze that question, it helps you figure out what service you were born to give. Life isn't just about taking away, it is also about contributions.

As we figure out what service we were created to give to others, it helps increase our self-worth because we are tapping into purpose. God specifically designs each of us to give some sort of service to others.

Then ask yourself: "What places do I like to go that makes me feel good inside?" When you analyze this question, then ask yourself: "What is it about this place that makes me feel happy?" As you explore these questions you will learn more about the environments you are most comfortable working in and going to. God wants us to have fun here on earth while we work in our area of purpose. Enjoy the people, places, and things He has given us, just don't make them your idols!

Other questions you are to ask yourself while you are getting to know "self" are the following:

- What are my favorite foods?
- What things do I like?
- What kind of people do I like to be around? Why?
- Who pushes me to perform my best?
- Who entertains me when they are around?
- What kind of music do I enjoy?
- What activities do I like to do?

As you begin to honestly evaluate your "self," you are essentially creating your road map for a happy, victorious life!

After we ascertain our likes, we are to analyze our dislikes. We do this by simply asking ourselves the same questions in reverse, which are below:

- What don't I enjoy doing?
- What things do I do that don't make me feel good about myself?
- What places do I go to that don't make me feel good inside?
- What foods don't I like?
- What things don't I like to do?
- What kind of people don't I like to be around? Why?
- Who in my life doesn't push me to perform my best?
- Who drains my energy when I have them around?
- What kind of music do I dislike?
- What activities do I hate to do?

By analyzing your dislikes, you are clearly able to see what things you need to avoid and what things you need to remove from your life. By participating in these activities and being around these people, you are essentially blocking your enjoyment. Everything about life is not going to be enjoyable, but we should avoid those things that do not add to our quality of life. We are unable to discard these things until we are able to come into consciousness of what they are. By spending time analyzing our dislikes, we create a definite scope of what we should avoid maintaining a happy, joyous lifestyle.

After we complete our analysis of "likes" and "dislikes," we must dig a little deeper and examine our strengths and weaknesses. This self-analysis becomes our road map for change.

We can only enjoy life based on the standards of our character. Our talents and abilities open the doorways to success, but we can only maintain that success with character. Without character, we are destined to self-destruct.

It's just like an eight year old who is given a brand-new car. The eight year old may very well have the ability to drive, yet he or she does not have the maturity to maintain the car. This lack of maturity will cause the eight year old to make inadequate decisions, which will ultimately lead to disaster! That is the same with us. We need character to maintain our success.

Character is developed by experience and getting to know "self." We must honestly be able to assess our strengths and weaknesses so we can work on building our character.

Each situation we experience in life gives us the chance to analyze our strengths and our weaknesses. We are to purposely study our experiences in meditation so we can assess the areas we need improvement. Each obstacle we endure exposes our character defects and our strengths. It is up to us to utilize our experiences as instruments or tools, which help us to advance.

When we study our experiences, we are able to make an accurate assessment of the things we need to change as well as the things we need to increase. When we utilize this process correctly, we constantly open the doors for growth and advancement.

Take the time to analyze yourself. Write down your strength and your weaknesses as you see them. Then sit down with at least three to four others who are close to you and whom you trust. Ask them to honestly tell you what they see your strengths and weaknesses are. Their viewpoint will help you get a clearer picture of what you need to work on in order to help improve "self."

Each day that you wake up, your priority should be becoming a greater "self." Life should be about the ways you can change course to ultimately improve "self." When you wake up in the morning, you should start your day by asking yourself two questions:

- What can I do today to improve "self?"
- What can I do today to take care of "self?"

Improving "self" is working on expanding your strength and enhancing your intellect, as well as working on strategies and techniques to decrease your character defects. Caring for "self" is doing the things that help you sustain your quality of life.

Gaining the wisdom and knowledge you need to soar helps sharpen your skill sets and abilities. Improving "self" is figuring out steps you can take to ultimately become a better "self."

Caring for "self" is the things that you do to sustain your enjoyment in life. Early in this chapter we discussed our "likes" and "dislikes". Caring for "self" is giving and performing for yourself the things which please you. It is taking pride and enjoyment in "self" and pampering "self" to remind "self" of its importance. It is our way of rewarding ourselves for being productive. For example, after you work hard doing the necessary things to improve your quality of life, stop and take time to allow yourself to enjoy a reward. If you like movies, rent one. If you like ice cream, treat yourself to a cone. If you like a certain theme park, buy yourself a ticket. Do things for yourself that you would like others to do for you by becoming your own lover!

Also, caring for "self" is maintaining good health and adequate grooming. If you fall apart, you are no good to anyone, especially yourself! Make sure you are eating the proper foods and exercising to maintain good health. It has been said if you exercise just fifteen minutes a day you could naturally lose up to eighteen pounds in a year! Watch your figure. How you look is very important. Take pride in your appearance. As you stare into the mirror and feel good about yourself, you will increase your self-esteem. High self-esteem is needed to soar through the billows of life! Create a schedule that includes maintaining proper health.

Your appearance is essential to your success. When you look good you tend to feel good about yourself. Take the time out to receive proper grooming. Do your hair and fix your nails and feet. Or treat yourself to the hair and nail salon and make an appointment at the spa. Get a facial and a massage. As you allow others to pamper you through their services, it helps you to feel good about yourself, and there are no strings attached. You pay them for their services, and your obligation is done.

Caring for "self" also includes getting the treatment and professional services you may need to help you sustain a good quality of life. Counseling can be a great instrument for improving "self." Oftentimes, people feel inadequate if they seek professional help, but the truth is, those who receive counseling tend to soar in life. Counselors help detect their patients' defects, which allows the person to clearly see what they need to work on. Unlike those who attend counseling, those who don't have trouble identifying their problems, so they go through life encountering the same situations, and not understanding why. If you are experiencing difficulties that are too great to handle, don't be ashamed to seek professional services, which include the assistance of a spiritual advisor. If you do, you will save a lot of time and gain wisdom on how to fix your dilemma.

Now that we know what we need to do to care for "self" and to improve "self," we must learn how to properly manage our time. In order to advance, we have to learn how to make the most of our time. When we are busy performing our everyday functions, it is hard to gain extra time to take care of and maintain "self." In order to create this needed time, we have to become conscious of those things that consume unnecessary space and time in our lives.

To overcome life's hurdles and obstacles, we must make "self" a priority. We do this by first analyzing how we have been consuming our time. Sit down and figure out how you utilize your time during the day. Take this schedule and figure out how you can create more time for "self." For example, on the way to work you can put in a self-help recording or inspirational message. On your lunch break you can go to the car and spend fifteen minutes in meditation. While taking the kids to an activity, you can bring a book that helps you work on self. Figure out the time slots and spaces where you can work on self-help strategies.

A lot of our time and energy is drained by people. The enemy uses people to help keep our focus off of purpose. Our love for people causes us to spend our time trying to help them change. The truth is, we cannot make people change. Change only occurs when a person is ready to change! "You can lead a horse to the well, but you can't make him (or her) drink," is a popular yet true statement. Many of us have based our happiness on people, so we become a magician, trying to perform tricks to make them happy, so we can be happy.

This pattern is purposeless. Remember, happiness comes from within! Until that person has a spiritual awakening, there is nothing you can do to help them! The biggest help you can give a person in that scenario is to walk away. Walking away from destructive, dysfunctional relationships is caring for "self." If a person is imposing on your quality of life, you must detach from them! If not, you will never be happy. That person's negative energy will always impose itself on you. The best advice I can give you, is to take a time out and separate! Use your time alone to work on "self."

Separation can have many positive effects. When you leave a relationship, your presence will be missed! A person is then able to see your true attributes. It also forces people to grow up and recognize their own shortcomings. If a relationship is meant to be, even if you separate, you both will come together again. This time hopefully, both parties will be whole. A relationship needs at least one whole person to help the other gain insight on the effectiveness of discovering God and purpose. When you are able to get yourself together, then and only then can you help someone else!

A big part of caring for "self" includes self-preservation. God has given us our bodies temporarily on earth, as gifts. It is our job to protect our gifts. We must not abuse our gifts, or let anyone else abuse them. We must stand up and make protecting "self" a priority! We protect "self" by considering ourselves before we make decisions and act on them. We evaluate each decision with the question: "Will this bring any harm to 'self?'" As we analyze this question, we begin to only allow things into our lives that benefit the well-being of "self." In essence, we become our own parent and friend. We open our eyes to the dangers around us and don't take risks that will endanger our protection. As we begin to protect "self," we gain a new sense of pride and self-worth.

The only way to protect "self" is to create boundaries. We build an invisible fence around ourselves that we don't allow people to cross. When others' activities impose on our own quality of life, we learn how to say no and simply walk away. We no longer feel obligated to people please; we get caught up into caring for the needs of "self." We learn our parameters and our areas of weaknesses. We do not let others enter those zones. We protect ourselves and avoid future mishaps.

Our time is very precious. We only get twenty-four hours each day, which we cannot increase. When we learn to care for "self," we no longer allow people to impose on our time. Our time becomes valuable and precious to us, so we value it. Therefore, we protect our peace. I am not saying we are not to help people. It's good to help people, but it is bad to disable people!

We disable others when we do the things for them that they should be doing for themselves. By creating boundaries, we no longer allow ourselves to take on the responsibilities of others. We allow others to grow by detaching and taking care of "self."

As we practice the principles of caring and improving self, through the law of attraction, we then signal others to begin to love and care for us! It is up to us to set the stage of what we will and will not allow! In essence, we must teach people how to treat us! As we begin to learn to love "self," we signal for others around us to share in our pursuit. People treat us the way we allow them to. By setting boundaries we no longer allow others to abuse us!

Have you ever seen a person who wasn't that attractive and really didn't have that much to offer, yet people flock to them and treat them like royalty? Now think about that person's attitude and how they treat their "self." It is their confidence and love of "self" that signals others to treat them in that same capacity. Essentially, they have tapped into the world for others to follow their course. The lesson here is: when we begin loving ourselves, we improve our quality of life and cause others to join in our mission!

In this chapter. we have learned a lot. We are coming to a close, but I want to reinforce and break down the strategies of the enemy of our souls. The enemy uses both spiritual and physical weapons to oppose us from reaching our divine destinies.

The spiritual weapons the enemy uses are thoughts that trigger fear, worry, and doubt. The physical weapons he uses are people. God sends people into our lives to help advance and enhance us. The enemy sends people into our lives to destroy us and distract us from fulfilling God's perfect plan.

Apart from caring for "self" is determining the people in our lives who are sent by God and those who are sent by the enemy. It is important that you analyze the purpose of those who you allow in your inner circle. Are they helpful, or are they a distraction? Do they enhance your life, if so in what way? Do they take away from your life, if so in what way? As we ask ourselves these necessary questions, we are able to ascertain those who were sent by God and those who were sent by the enemy. This is a process we should perform periodically in our lives.

If a person was sent in our lives by the enemy, no matter how much we love them, they will never be productive to us, unless this person has a spiritual awakening. The chances of a person having a spiritual awakening who is being used by the enemy is very slim. Most likely, they don't have a clue that they are even being used!

Have you ever let a person go, or maybe they walked out of your life, and at first you were hurt and upset? Then after a little time, you gained back your strength and started to do really well without them? Suddenly, this person reappears in your life and you accept them back, then your life goes downhill again. This is a sign that this person was sent in your life strategically by the enemy to destroy you! Their hidden mission is destruction.

God has so many wonderful gifts to give us, but His gifts are intended to bring us joy. He does not bless us for us to give His gifts to people whom He doesn't desire to have them. Just as we have to work hard and do the right things to be rewarded, so do these people. When we offer our God-given blessing to undeserving people, He begins to dry up our wells. In the places we used to store abundance, we will find ourselves with very little. This obstacle is created to show us we do, in fact, have human termites in our lives. The only way to overcome this obstacle is to get rid of them. Getting rid of these people is a part of caring for "self." You must care for "self" to receive ultimate fulfillment and happiness out of life!

If you are ready to make a change and do what is necessary to begin to care for "self," follow me in this short prayer for guidance:

"Dear God, I thank You for bringing me into awareness of the need to begin to care for 'self.' I ask You to open my eyes and help me see the beauty you created in me. Expose my hidden gifts and talents to me and lead me onto the road of purpose. Each day give me the desire to work on improving my relationship with You and working on "self." Help me clearly see those things I need to change and give me the insight on how to change them. Help me to always be content with the perfect way that You have designed me. Help me to find the fulfillment I've been looking for while I spend time with You. Open my eyes to the insight I need to rid myself of the people, places, and things that have been destructive to my life. Help me to manage my time wisely, allowing each of my days here on earth to be productive.

I now thank You for your help and your guidance and receive your strength. Amen."

Congratulations! You have successfully completed another huge step. Study this chapter and master the techniques you have learned. Learning to care for "self" is a process, but it will ultimately change your quality of life for the better! Like the other techniques, you must practice them to master them. It will take time and discipline, but you can do it!

Stay focused and continue on your journey. You still have a little way to go. Before you know it, what you thought was an obstacle will become your stairway to your greatest success!

QUESTIONS

1. Why is comparing yourself to society's standards destructive?
2. How can people-pleasing take you away from your purpose?
3. Why must people be whole to have a successful relationship?
4. What measures can you take to learn about yourself?
5. What is improving "self," and what is caring for "self?" How do they differ?
6. Why is professional help good to receive at times?
7. What is the difference between the people God sends into our lives and the people the enemy sends?

WRITING ASSIGNMENT

Write out your analysis of likes and dislikes. Also write out your analysis of your character defects and strengths.

Do your interviews with three to four of your trusted friends or family members and write out their findings of what your strengths and character defects are.

Conclude this writing assignment with your analysis of people, places, and things that are good for you and those that are not. Also create a one-week self-care schedule, including all the things you will do for that week to care for self.

VII. TAPPING INTO YOUR PURPOSE

POINT 7:

"Life without a mission is empty, dull, and worthless! In order to find fulfillment, I must discover my purpose!"

Many of us have gotten lost in the billows of life, trying hard to attain self-fulfillment. It has been our belief that our inner void can be satisfied by external things and worldly accomplishments. Our entire being became filled with passion, eagerly pursuing our search for fulfillment. We searched high and low, looking for the things we believed would bring us ultimate satisfaction. We searched for people, possessions, recognition and accomplishments, believing they would fill our low self-esteem. We quickly dropped one unfulfilling thing to pursue another. Our search intensified as we believed we were coming closer and closer to finally obtaining our mark. After many toils and intensive work, some of us even accomplished our mission. We obtained the rewards we lusted for, believing we now possessed the very thing that would fulfill us, only to discover in our prize of achievement, there was no fulfillment at all!

Disappointed by our pointless journey, many of us became discouraged. Some had the faith to begin again and continued the same hopeless cycles. Others became beaten down by depression and looked for a way of escape through alcohol and drugs. Today, we are here by divine appointment, to break the unsuccessful cycles of man's search for meaning. We no longer have to stay empty and void! Today, we can access the true key to fulfillment!

In this chapter, we will learn how to tap into the power of purpose. We will discuss vital points, which will help us reshape our perceptions of life, its meaning and purpose. By the end of this chapter, we will have a clearer picture of what our greatest enjoyment here on earth should be, causing it to become our actual experience!

To understand life and ascertain its meaning, we must develop a strong belief system. By getting to know our "Higher Power" and his attributes, we discover his purposes for man on earth. As we read our holy book, we are able to discover the patterns of God and the ways of man. This discovery opens our eyes to the reason we were all created.

Our creator is perfect, He makes no mistakes. Each of us was designed by God with His unique plan in mind. A common misconception is: Life is all about "self." When we learn about God and His plan, we discover life is really all about God! Each of us were created for God`s perfect purpose!

God is our Creator and our Father. He has many children in all shapes, colors, and creeds. It is God's desire that His children operate together as a family, in love. In God`s family we all have different attributes and assignments. It is God's desire that we work together in love, creating a family in union. Each of us were created to perform a task or to complete an assignment on earth that benefits God's family. As we each perform our duties and tasks, we help the betterment of the entire whole. Therefore, our purpose on earth is service! When we perform this service, we give honor to God. When God is honored, he honors us! As our creator and our designer, He knows just what will satisfy us. As God is pleased with us, He rewards us with fulfillment. True fulfillment only comes from God!

Finding purpose is learning how to surrender to God's will for our lives. When we stop being stubborn and come to the realization that we cannot make it on our own, we are able to open our hearts to follow God's lead. God is a gentleman; He will not force us to be led by him. However, He sends storms to expose to us the reality of our weakness, yet it is up to us to choose to accept His guidance.

Surrendering to God is simply saying, "God, I trust you" You may not understand why He allows certain circumstances to happen as they do, but always remember, God is all knowing! Not only does he know what's happening today, God knows what will happen tomorrow. Our journey in life is preparation for all those things we must undergo in the future, which will lead us to purpose. We are constantly training for what is yet to come. As we spend time getting to know our "Higher Power," His ways, and His attributes, we open up the doors of our hearts to trust that His plan is always best. As we put aside our own plans and pick up the wisdom of God, we move out of our own way and become guided by God into purpose.

As a successful real estate investor, I thought I was good. I never thought about purpose or even analyzed my gifts and talents. My focus was getting to the money. I always helped others, but not in the manner I was created to. My incarceration led me to my purpose. I never even knew I had a gift to write, or that I was created to minister to others through my outreach. When I finally had this discovery and started walking in my purpose, the inner feeling I received inside was like nothing I ever experienced before. When God was pleased with me, I felt it in the deepest part of my spirit. This feeling actually fueled me to do things I never dreamed or imagined. That can be your fate, too, when you tap into your purpose!

Many of us have been heavily involved in the cat and dog race of the world, looking for fulfillment. As we surrender to God's plan, life becomes less chaotic. We are no longer fighting against God. Purpose ultimately simplifies our life. Just as a parent no longer has to discipline a child who behaves properly, God will no longer send the same trials and tribulations to get our attention. Once we pass our test, we can move on to the next level or another phase of life.

As we discussed in Chapter 2, God doesn't intend to be our enemy. God desires to be our Partner and Friend. In order to accomplish His tasks here on earth, He utilizes the service of people. As God develops trusts with His servants, He forms partnerships with them. He gives His human partners strength, intellect, and knowledge to perform duties here on earth. When God becomes our Partner, we can perform exploits by His power! All inventions and powerful resources created here on earth come through the divine assistance of God. Remember, God is all knowing! When we allow God to use us in partnership as His vessels, we gain divine insight that enables us to do things we could not do in our human strength. God puts His super on our natural and we, as His partners, are able to perform supernatural task here on earth!

As we tap into our purpose and begin to work in our service to God, our fulfillment is obtained. Our service becomes our offering to God. It shows Him we love Him, and we trust Him. Working in our purpose is ultimately our worship and honor to God. As we please Him in worship, He blesses us! God has many gifts stored up for His children, and God's gifts come without sorrow. He knows just what to give us at the perfect time. No one can please us better than God can! As we begin in our service to God, we open the doors of abundance and prosperity!

God is love. It is His greatest desire for his friends and servants to be filled with love. Love gives and expects nothing in return. Love is kind and merciful. Love looks after the best interest of others as it cares for itself. Love is peaceful and gentle. Love is longsuffering and patient. Love is faithful and loyal, just as it is full of joy. These are the attributes God intends for us to have while we are performing our service to Him.

When working in purpose, it's important to understand we are working for God and not people. God is our rewarder, and *not* man. When we give to others, we are performing our service to God. We are doing what we are called to do. We are not to look to man to provide for us, we are to understand that with God, it is not like at a job. We are not working to receive man's compensation or man's reward. We are working to honor God and to receive the rewards He has already planned to give us. Therefore, our work is not based on how man treats or honors us. Our work is done to please our Partner, which is the one who sent us. Our work then becomes our worship to God.

When God gives us a plan, He provides us with provision. We don't have to be crafty in our human wisdom and manipulate the scales. When we begin to work in purpose, God will ultimately send us the right people, places, and things we need in order to accomplish our mission! We can trust that God will supply for whatever He commissions.

Lack of provision is a sign that we are out of the will of God. Financial hardships caution us that we are headed in the wrong direction. That is not to say we will never have financial troubles. All of us at some point in our lives face financial struggles, but when there are constant issues with provision, we have to examine our lives to see if we are out of alignment with God`s purpose.

You know when you are working in your purpose because you begin to feel fulfilled. Working in your purpose gives you a high greater than you could ever imagine! You feel an inner sense of self-worth—that you are doing the right thing. This is because when God is proud of us, He stirs up our emotions with His joy. In essence, when we are working in our purpose, we know we have found it, because God allows us to feel His special joy inside! This is His way of motivating us to continue functioning in this capacity. God's joy brings us strength that is incomparable to human strength. The joy He sends stirs up our will and desire. It causes us to be more productive.

When we work in our purpose, we don't dread working. We enjoy it! Whether we receive compensation or not, we perform with the same passion, no longer motivated by our inner joy. When we work in our purpose, it brings us and those we serve, great pleasure. Our work then becomes an expression of love.

The talent God has given us to perform our special tasks must be given as a gift or service to God's desired recipients here on earth. As we work in purpose, we become God's vessel on earth that He uses to distribute His gifts onto others. When we give our gift of service, it must be done in love! In order to work properly in our purpose, we must do so with the correct heart and right motives. If what we have given is not given with the right spirit, then it is not a gift at all! God doesn't just put His trust in us based on what we say or what we promise. Instead God tests us through trials to expose what our heart is really made of. He wants to see our character and what is inside of our hearts. God wants to make sure we possess the necessary ingredients to perform His desired task. As we pass our tests by overcoming the hurdles of life with faithfulness, loyalty, and gratitude to God, He will begin to trust us with His gifts. The more strength we gain, the greater our blessings become!

These blessings are not intended for us to hoard. God gives us gifts to bless others. We then become vehicles God uses to disperse His gifts to others. Purpose is not all about "self;" it is about love, God, and His family. The greater our love becomes, the more fulfillment we will receive!

Many of us have been experiencing storms and we`ve cried, feeling as though God has abandoned us. We don't understand why we are going through what we are going through. We look at ourselves, and in our hearts, we know we are good people. We see others around us who are evil, yet they seem to be experiencing joy; this leaves us in further confusion. We begin to believe God doesn't love us, or that he is punishing us. Our belief is sincerely incorrect! The people on earth that God chooses to utilize and honor, He tests. In this case, He is sending the storms to get us in line and prepared for the mission He has for us. He knows we are good people and that is why He chooses us. He also knows we will remain faithful and pass the test! God doesn't want us to get caught up in the world's system. He stirs us up to get our eyes off the world so we will put our focus on Him. Some of the most compassionate people in this world are those who have experienced wretched trials and tribulations. Life`s storm have humbled them and opened their eyes to what's most important in life. As God showed these people His love during their tribulations, these same people now know how to show others the same love. They then spread the love of God to those in need, spiraling a new cycle of God`s love here on earth.

It is no coincidence that you are at this place at this time. God no longer wants you to run around in circles, chasing your tail. He doesn't want you to serve people, places, and things, making them your idols, to only in the end be disappointed and unfulfilled. This is the season that God wants you to develop a relationship with Him, and in turn discover your purpose! It is God's greatest pleasure to see you happy and fulfilled in every aspect of your life. The key to tapping into this joy is seeking Him and discovering His plan for your life. No longer delay your journey! Concentrate and use this season to figure out what things matter the most. The obstacle you are enduring has a purpose; it has been sent to lead you to the very place you are at today. Surrender your own plan that has failed you in numerous ways and pick up God's divine plan that has been shaped even before your existence!

All the exercises we have previously done in this book has helped lead us to this point. We learned how to create a partnership with our "Higher Power," how to meditate, and how to take the time out to learn and care for "self." In the previous chapter, we began to learn about our likes and our dislikes, as well as our talents and abilities. Now we are ready to use this information to help us tap into our purpose! Remember, our purpose is the service we give back to God. It is our expression of love here on earth that benefits others. Purpose is not about self and self-fulfillment; it is about serving God and performing the tasks He desires us to do here on earth.

The first question to ask when searching for your purpose is what service do I provide that people benefit from most that can bring God glory? We have to dig within and recount our most pleasurable experiences where we were able to do something special for someone else that made them feel good and made us feel good too. As we explore these experiences, we are led into our path of purpose.

As children, we all have dreams within our hearts. These desires are given to us by God. As a child, what did you desire to do when you got older? Are you now pursing that dream? If not, there is a chance that you have been operating outside of your purpose. Now is the time to dig deep in your heart and figure out what you can do that will bring you ultimate joy and fulfillment, yet at the same time, please God. Make it your goal and your mission to seek God in prayer and pursue this dream! It is never too late! You can always begin again and take the necessary steps to rehash your dreams. If you don't, you will ultimately remain unfulfilled. God is merciful! He gives each of us a chance to pursue purpose, but we all have an expiration period. If God sees that we don't intend to use the skills and talents he entrusts us with, he begins to prune the tree, getting rid of all dead weight. Don't let the time clock expire. Take out the time and strength to pursue your purpose!

Going back in time and replaying our life experiences during meditation opens the door for us to find our purpose. Nothing in life happens by chance! Each experience we have had, both bad and good, play a part in leading us to purpose. As we replay our experiences during meditation, our areas of compassion are revealed. We discover the very places where we desire to give service in helping others overcome the obstacles we were able to get through. Our experiences ultimately lead us to the area God wishes us to work. He exposes us to a problem, then He gives us compassion to help others overcome it.

Each of us has a unique personality that was created to help us serve in our purpose. Before your existence, as God equipped you, he distinctively made you the way that you are. It is your personality that will be used to demonstrate God's love to someone else who is in need. It is important that you examine every component of your being, so you can discover where you excel at the most. This discovery will bring you closer to discovering your purpose.

I have given you the basic points about purpose, what to look for in discovering purpose, and how to find it. Now I will share with you my personal testimony of how I came in alignment with my purpose. I don't claim to be an expert as there are still many undiscovered aspects of my purpose. I am an overcomer and a person who has experienced a numerous amount of successes as well as failures. It is my rough experiences in life that led me to the place where I am today in spiritual maturity. I share my story to provide you with my map to purpose, which you can use and compare to your own life experiences.

I grew up in Jamaica, Queens in an African American middle-class home. My parents were very poor growing up, and they struggled to overcome the hardships of poverty. They migrated from Kinston, North Carolina to Jamaica Queens to make a better life for their family. My parents wanted their children to obtain all the things they were unable to obtain being poor. My mother enrolled me in all types of activities. From a young age I swam, played tennis, did judo, danced, sang, and pursued acting. By the time I was ten years old, I traveled the country performing in an off Broadway hit show. I began to obtain money at an early age and developed a very competitive nature.

Growing up, many of my peers became successful in the hip-hop music industry, becoming famous executives, rap artists, and DJ's. I admired their fame and ability to make money, so I started servicing their financial needs to break into the business. I started off helping them obtain houses and cars, and later got involved in helping close substantial business deals. As a result, I began to make a lot of money and gained significant prestige amongst my peers.

From a young age, I was involved in the church and had a love for God, which never left me. As I began to make more and more money, I stayed away from God and unconsciously started serving my new idol, money.

During my early twenties, I got heavily involved in real estate and made several million dollars, feeling as if was finally fulfilled because I obtained my goal of making money. I lived a very luxurious lifestyle, and I was in the crowd of the who's who. I drove fancy cars and dressed in the finest clothes. I had everything I worked so desperately to obtain, yet I was lonely and miserable inside.

Then I came up with the bright idea that I needed companionship. My next pursuit became the search for a male companion. I passionately pursued my chase, thinking I could create the perfect male for me. I used my money to lure in what I perceived to be the best of mates, only to discover my efforts backfired on me. The more I gave, the more obligated my companions made me feel. They never loved me; they only loved the things I could provide for them. When my money left, they quickly dispersed too!

During my pursuit of fulfillment, I became the target of an FBI investigation. My passion for money led to me compromise my integrity in my business dealings. I was what you might call a "tweaker," one who manipulates the system to get what they need quicker. Instead of slowing down and getting where I was destined to go in God's own timing, I manipulated my way to the top. All I saw was my goal, which led me to be blinded to consequences.

My obstacles and misfortunes brought me back to God. I became highly involved in church and found it to be an outlet of escape from my problems. I met a pastor who helped me tap into my passion for ministry, and I devoted myself into helping our church purchase a new building.

During my time giving service, I achieved great fulfillment. I finally felt as though my life had great purpose and meaning. The time I spent at the church built up my faith tremendously. Just when I thought I was finally in the place I needed to be, an overzealous FBI agent decided to make me a part of his target practice. Even though I was no longer even involved in real estate, my lifestyle and the high-profile celebrities I associated with, roused the attention of this agent, who ultimately became obsessed with me. I was locked up a total of six times all by the same agent. Most of the charges were for fabricated things I was unaware of.

Even through my legal struggles, I received multiple other challenges that I didn't understand. On July 16, 2008, I was sentenced to 151 months in Federal prison, with still two Federal court cases and one state case pending. I traveled across the country in handcuffs and shackles for close to two years fighting legal battles. As a single 31 year old mother, separated from her children, I went from New York, to Oklahoma, from California back to Connecticut, traveling on smelly buses and run down planes from one destination to another. I desperately wanted to close my eyes and give up on life, but something inside wouldn't allow me to.

Instantly, I became the ridicule of my peers. Left deserted, only my family was there to support me during my struggles. While imprisoned, I sought wisdom and knowledge passionately. Each day I spent hours reading and spending time with God, trying to understand why all this was happening to me. In my cell I got a breakthrough and learned the purpose of my troubles.

My analysis led me to discover my first mistake occurred when I made money my idol. I placed money before God, allowing myself to be led by it. When money became my idol, I became blinded to my true purpose, which I felt at the time was to pursue money. Nevertheless, my passion was always to help people. I helped my peers pursue their goals and ascertain assets. I had a natural talent to motivate people, yet I used this skill for my purpose and not God's. I pursued money and men, who both became my idols, not realizing God would never let me be happy and sustain the things in my life that I put before Him!

My obstacles led me back to the place where God wanted me to be, on my knees, looking to Him. My battles were severe and very intense because my skills and talents led me to believe I could control and manipulate events to work in my favor. It took me a long time to learn how to surrender my will and operate according to God's will. I thought it might be something I didn't want, so I fought against it. The longer I fought, the more intense my battles became!

In my lonely cell, stripped away of all my idols, I created a solid relationship with my "Higher Power," who led me to my purpose. I began to create self-help books that have been very essential in helping others who have experienced great obstacles in life. I received no greater pleasure than to have my readers tell me how my writings had helped them change their outlook and their course in life. Their words reminded me that there was purpose in my pain!

At the worst place I believed I could be in my life, I found my greatest discovery. I can truthfully say, I am no longer wrapped in spiritual chains; my spirit is free. As I learned to surrender to God and let Him bring out the best of me!

My story isn't over, but the key is for me to stay in alignment with my purpose. That which I never imagined I was strong enough to endure, I am able to handle because I am now in tune with God. He is the source of my strength! You are no different from me. You can also gain the strength you need to outlast the storm! Finding strength comes when you find your purpose!

Are you ready to tap into your purpose and discover God`s intent for your life? Well, follow me in this prayer for purpose:

"Dear God, I thank You for new enlightenment. I no longer want to pursue the worldly cycle of fulfillment. Today, I understand that the system is pointless! I know I will never be fulfilled until I come into alignment with Your perfect plan for my life. I know I was placed on this earth to serve You, by serving others. Help me to discover the exact assignment You created for me. Help me surrender my will and take up Your will for my life.

Open my eyes to understanding so I can meditate and receive the revelations I need to complete my journey. Illuminate my spiritual gifts, abilities, and talents and allow me to see the purpose for my life's experiences. Today, I know that You love me and have not sent my obstacles to hurt me, but You sent them to lead me into purpose. So, today, I give myself wholeheartedly to You. Use me as You wish to carry out your plan here on earth. You are my Father and my Creator. I am your servant, your partner, and most importantly your friend. I thank You now for leading me into my purpose. Amen."

Wow! You have crossed another major benchmark. The doors of purpose have now swung open in your life! It's up to you to walk through them! Congratulations! Stay focused and continue in your mission! You have entered the pathway of purpose.

QUESTIONS

1. Why is life without purpose void?
2. Why do we need a strong belief system to discover purpose?
3. What's the difference between serving God and serving self?
4. What does it mean to surrender to God?
5. Why is finding purpose fulfilling?
6. How do we discover our purpose? How do we express God's love?
7. Why are our life experiences vital in helping us discover purpose?

WRITING ASSIGNMENT

Utilize the analysis charts you created in the last chapter. Examine them and then write out what service you believe you can offer God that is aligned with His intended purpose for you.

VIII. GIVING BACK

POINT 8:

"If I choose to be selfish, I'll always suffer from lack. To open the doors of abundance, I must learn how to give back."

From as early on as I can remember, I loved to share and giveback to others. Seeing the smile on a person's face whom I blessed meant everything to me. My parents taught me to share and I did it with ease. At the time, I didn't realize my sharing was setting me up for bigger blessings.

Although giving back to others is a universal principle that sets in motion receiving in abundance, for many of us we have never been taught how to properly give back, which can be detrimental. In my case, I blessed many people with things they were not supposed to have. From luxury cars that my so-called "friends" could not afford, to down payments for homes that my children would later on not be welcomed into, I gave people things they didn't deserve. Those actions backfired on me. I guess in a sense I was playing the role of God in people's lives and that wasn't my place.

Consequently, the people who I gave the most too often flipped on me. Truth is, when you give people things they didn't work for and you become familiar with them, they begin to secretly despise you. They are able to see you are just like them, yet you have the things they wish they could have for themselves. Some of my worst hits came from intimate partners, whose affection turned from gratitude to resentment.

Life experience taught me why it's so important to make sure those in your immediate circle are equally yoked, not just financially but spiritually, too. I also learned how to sow seeds of time or service, instead of money and how to teach others to earn on their own, rather than me doing all of the work. With these lessons learned, I felt it was important to share a chapter on how to properly give back.

To be prosperous in life we must learn the principle of giving back. Most people would say, "Oh, that's simple. I always help people." The truth of the matter is, often what we do for people that we perceive as helping them, is actually hurting them. That type of help is not considered giving back!

As we discussed in the previous chapter, we are all a part of God's wonderful family. As a family member, we are all required to be productive and give back to support our family. We cannot expect to eat off the great table of life, if we don't take part in helping prepare the feast. Our help can be given in various forms. Through this journey, we have been learning how to tap into our gifts and our talents, as well as our skill sets and abilities. As we begin to discover "self," we must learn in which capacity we wish to contribute to God`s family here on earth.

According to the Universal Law of Reciprocity, the more we give, the more we will receive. As we make a concentrated effort to give back, He will open the doors of prosperity. This means the more we give back to God, the greater our opportunities and experiences will be in life!

Some people believe if they obtain something or gain knowledge, it should be kept for themselves. It is human nature to be selfish. People are afraid that others will advance above them, especially if they teach what they know, so they hoard their skills, talents, and abilities. This is against God's principles!

God blessed us with gifts and talents, so we can share them with His family. The more gifts and talents He entrusts us with, the more we are required to give back. He blesses us so we can enjoy His blessings, but God's blessings are not just for ourselves and our immediate family. God wants us to open our hearts and give to our universal family too! We give to our universal family by finding ways to offer our gifts and talents back to the universe!

In this chapter, we will learn different ways to assess how we can be more productive in our giving, so receiving in abundance automatically follows! It is God's law! Just as the law of gravity says, if we jump in the air we will not stay afloat, but we will come back down to the ground. The law of reciprocity says, as we give, more will come back to us. This law lets us know how essential giving is to receiving prosperity. Remember, the world's richest people are the world's biggest givers! God delights in blessing us when He can trust us to give back to our Universal Family!

When we work in our field of purpose, it is okay to receive compensation for our work. For example, God may call a gift something we give that is of value, that we expect nothing in return for. If we receive compensation for our gift, then it is not a gift at all! That makes it a mutual agreement.

You are not expected to work for free. God gives us talents so we can make money and care for ourselves. However, in addition to the services we are compensated for, we are also required to give back. Our giving back is a gift to God; in return, God compensates us by opening different outlets and doors for us here on earth!

To be prosperous, we must purposely figure out what gifts we can offer God on earth. These gifts can be given in three forms, our service, our time, or our money.

When we offer our service to God, we utilize our skill sets and talents to help bless someone in need. For example, the doctor who is compensated for his services may offer a free clinic to disadvantaged people, one weekend a month. The doctor doesn't receive any compensation for his services, so his service becomes his gift back to God. God will ultimately compensate the doctor for his gift of service.

When we offer our gift of service, we must do it with a heart of love. God wishes us to take on His spirit of love as we serve others in need. As we care for individuals through our offering of service, they should feel the power of our genuine love and compassion. Our love then radiates to the heart of the individuals we serve, sparking hope and faith within them. In essence, they feel as if God is shining His light upon them, and they receive our service as God's personal gift to them. That is the type of gift that gets God's attention! As we give with the spirit of love, God rewards us greatly. His rewards then become God's way of saying, "My good and faithful servant, job well done!"

Our gift of service can include any skill set or talent we are good at. For example, a singer can perform a free concert, a janitor can sweep the floors of a homeless shelter without pay, a lawyer can give free legal services to the needy, and a child can help their elderly neighbor carry their groceries. Whatever your skill set is, no matter how small or how great, you can offer your gift of service to God, and He will reward you! God constantly seeks those He can use to help support His Universal Family! The problem is, so many of us are concentrating only on helping ourselves, not realizing this selfish behavior only keeps us stagnant.

Our gift to God can include our time. We can donate our time to others and become a blessing to them. There are many people in the world who are lonely and wish to talk to someone. We can take time out and spend it with others who are in need. This becomes our expression of love.

For example, you can go to a boys or girls club and donate your time to kids there. You can go to a nursing home and volunteer your time to the elderly. You can also go to the homeless shelter and offer your time there. When we give our time to others in need, expecting no compensation in return, we are offering God our gift of time! Just as with our gift of service, we must give our time with love. The recipient should feel that our gift of time was sent to them directly from God. As we offer our gift of time, we brighten the heart of the recipient, which causes God to brighten our own hearts! Our gifts to others benefit us just as greatly as those who receive them!

Another gift we are required to give God is money. Biblically, we are required to give God a tenth of everything we make. That equals ten cents off of each dollar we make. This gift becomes our offering of appreciation. When we show God appreciation and thanksgiving, it causes Him to return appreciation and thanksgiving back to us. God loves a cheerful giver!

When we offer our money to God, we give it to others in need, looking for no compensation in return. This money can be given to organizations that help the needy, or to individuals who are in need. It is our personal choice on how we give our gifts back to God. Just as we take our time picking out a gift for someone we deeply love, we should take our time and carefully figure out how and what we will give God. When we take out the time to plan our giving back to God, we show our appreciation and admiration for all He has done. God desires us to love Him. Our gift to God is a reflection of our love for Him. The more love we show God, the more love He will offer back to us!

Giving back to God helps remind us of the reason we were placed on earth. It helps us take our minds off self and place our minds on God and purpose. God has wired each of us to feel fulfilled when we operate in the function of giving. This action helps satisfy us within. It fuels our lives with purpose and meaning.

As we share with others and they show their gratitude and appreciation, it makes us feel happy and worthy inside. Giving also causes the person whose life has been touched to want to join in on the cycle. They too begin to give! That makes giving contagious. God's desire is for all of His children here on earth to join in the cycle of giving. When we give, we help eliminate lack within the universe. The cycle of giving creates plenty for everyone!

It is the heart of compassion that produces effective change on earth. When we operate out of love, we possess the power to heal and restore. The greatest change that takes place on earth is out of hearts filled with love.

We learned through this journey that obstacles often come our way, so that we will have compassion for others. God lets us go through things and overcome them, so we can help someone else do the same thing. A good way to discover our purpose is to spend time analyzing our areas of pain.

The hardships we endure lead us into purpose. After we overcome our hurdles, we then become qualified to teach others how to do likewise! In order to receive, we must sow good seeds. While going through hardships, one of the greatest remedies is to spend time figuring out what gifts you can offer to God. As we help others, we take our minds off our problems and open the door of help to come in return directly from God.

Now that we understand the essentials of giving back, let's explore the difference between giving to individuals and giving to God.

Many of us have gotten caught up into giving to individuals, because we are programmed to feel a sense of fulfillment when we do something good for others. God created us to give, so when we express our love to others by giving, we feel good inside. It gives us a sense of pride and self-worth. This feeling has caused many of us to misuse our gifts to create this sense of fulfillment. These feelings cause us to do more and more for these selective recipients. We then thrive off the idea that we are needed by them, and their need for us gives a false sense of self-worth. Over time we find ourselves becoming codependent, relying on the need to be needed by these individuals. Consequently, these individuals begin to control our lives based on the emotions they share with us, or their lack of sharing! We become reliant on their praise to fill up our inner void. In essence, this type of giving back is not genuine, because we are looking for something in return.

We care for these individuals, expecting them to give us their love and gratitude in return. The idolizing of their love soon follows! We do whatever it takes to receive their praise and affection. We consume our lives with figuring out ways we can get them to love us more. Our self-worth then becomes dependent on their feelings for us. We, for all intents and purposes, have subconsciously made these people our idols. Remember, anything or anyone we give more time to thank God, becomes our idol. Also, anyone we rely on instead of God, becomes an idol as well.

God is a jealous God! He will always cause friction between us and our idols. God will never allow those things and people we put before Him to fulfill us. Our inner void can only be filled by God!

When we give to individuals, we tend to believe we are helping them, but in fact when we do for them what they should be doing for themselves, we disable them! These people then become reliant upon us instead of relying on God for their provision. We in turn become that person's idol too! We've already learned whatever we idolize God will destroy! We can cause our own self destruction when we allow people to make us their idols. God will then make our work toward them unfruitful in order to destroy their idolatry toward us. Instead of loving us and admiring what we do for them, they will begin to despise and resent us.

Have you ever done a lot for a person to gain their love and trust, only for them to be unappreciative and stab you in the back in return? You cry and complain to yourself, not understanding why they treat you as they do. Why? God has allowed this obstacle to occur to create dissension between this person and yourself. This dissension is created to open both of your eyes to an ungodly relationship. Wherever we build up idols in our lives, they will be torn down! It might not happen today, but it will eventually occur tomorrow. Constantly evaluate your life to see if you have opened the doors to idolatry. Immediately uproot all idols by turning your focus back to God!

When we give to God by offering our service to people, we do not disable them. We don't provide for people who are capable of providing for themselves. We help the needy and disadvantaged people that God places on our hearts to help. Once we give, we don't expect anything in return. We have no hidden agenda or motive for our gift. It is simply our offering to God.

The greatest thing we can offer a person is empowering them to provide for themselves. Instead of giving a person something, we take the time to show them how they can provide it for themselves. We share our wisdom and knowledge with that person, so they don't just eat today; we empower them to eat for life!

When we provide mentorship to others, we provide them with the gift of empowerment. As stated earlier, many people are afraid to share what they know with others. They selfishly hoard their skills, and this, in essence, blocks their blessings. As we share our skill sets with God, we open the doors for God to trust us with more wisdom. It also causes those we mentor to join in our cycle of giving. They in turn take the information we give them and pass it on to others. When God looks down from heaven and notices His universal family is working in unison, He receives praise and honor from us.

It's time to go inside our closets of "self" and figure out what gifts we can give back to God. What has God blessed you with that can be of great value to someone else? It's time to do a spring cleaning and make use of some of the things we have stored on our shelves. Already, we have made several assessments of our skills and our talents in the last couple of chapters. Now it's time to take our analyses and figure out how we can give back to God.

In this last section, I will provide you with some examples of people who decided to give back to God by giving to others. Compare these examples to your own life, so you can figure out how best to utilize your gifts.

EXAMPLE 1:

Sheila graduated from college with honors. She worked hard to become a teacher and got promoted to become a principal of a prominent school. Sheila was doing great in life until she met Bill. He was a janitor and aspiring singer, who worked at her school. Bill won Sheila over with his charm, and the two began to date. Sheila noticed Bill was having financial problems and decided to offer her assistance by letting him move in. Bill moved into Sheila's luxury condo and fell in love with his newfound lifestyle. As a result, Bill began to shower Sheila with the love and attention she always sought after. Things started off great, or so Sheila thought!

After a few months, Bill decided to quit his job and pursue his singing career at Sheila's expense. After a while, Bill was no longer charming to Sheila; he became an extra liability! Sheila had to cook, clean, and pay all the bills with no assistance from Bill. Afraid of being alone, Sheila tolerated Bill's behavior, hoping one day he would make it big and sell lots of music.

As Bill started performing at more venues and got the attention of women, he started cheating and treated Sheila badly. He would often insult her about her weight and even told her that she was going nowhere in life.

One night, Bill came home drunk after performing at a club, and he beat Sheila and accused her of cheating. The stress got so intense that Sheila started making drastic mistakes at her job and was threatened with termination by her superiors.

After seeking counseling, Sheila decided to break up with Bill. She took out a restraining order and had the police escort Bill out of her home. Based on the therapist's recommendation, Sheila sought a spiritual journey to help herself heal from the pain of Bill, who despite his downfalls, Sheila greatly missed.

Sheila decided while she was healing from Bill she would give back to God. She prayed to her "Higher Power" for a way to honor Him in her service. Sheila was given the divine idea to start a free afterschool program at her school that would focus on bringing up the academic levels of the students.

Sheila was successful at getting many teachers in the school involved, and they jointly donated their time to the students two days a week. As a result, many of the students soared during state-wide testing, and Sheila was praised by her superiors for her work and her ethics.

Eventually, Sheila got so caught up in her students that she forgot all about Bill. One day *Newsweek* decided to do a story on Sheila, and a handsome reporter was assigned to interview her. Sheila and the reporter hooked up, and shortly thereafter, they got married. Sheila now enjoys a great life with her new husband and is currently expecting her first child.

Take notice, Sheila's life was going well until she met Bill. His love and affection toward Sheila caused her to make Bill her idol. As Bill began to soar, she got to see his true colors. God opened Sheila's eyes by allowing Bill to mistreat her. Sheila was devastated, believing that this was the worst obstacle she could go through. After Sheila sought professional help and was led onto her path of restoration, Sheila learned the importance of giving back and got caught up in her service to God. In turn, God rewarded Sheila for her service. He allowed her to excel and gain back the good graces of her superiors, as well as rewarded her with a husband who is good to her. Sheila is no different from you and I! As we get more involved in giving back, we open God's heart of abundance!

EXAMPLE 2:

Johnathan grew up in a poor rural town in the South, raised by good Christian parents, who often prayed for him. Johnathan desperately wanted to overcome poverty and move his parents to a better place. He had a great skill for playing basketball; he worked hard at sharpening his skills daily. As a result, Johnathan excelled in high school basketball and was drafted to the NBA.

Johnathan was able to achieve his dream, and he moved his parents into a wonderful home in Florida.

Although Johnathan was an average-looking male, his newfound riches caused many women to flock to him. Johnathan was solicited by this beautiful woman named Carla who was very advanced in seducing men. She quickly boosted Johnathan's confidence. When he was with

Carla he felt like a king. She would play on his ego and compliment him every chance she got, and he began to feel special. As a direct result, Johnathan showered Carla with gifts. He bought her diamonds, fur coats, and even a new car.

Johnathan's mother didn't like Carla, even though Carla was very nice to her. She knew something was not right with son's lover but couldn't pinpoint it. She urged Johnathan to be careful, but he wouldn't listen. After his mother's constant nagging, Johnathan decided to disconnect from his mother.

Carla was happy. She moved in with Johnathan and began controlling his life. She got rid of anyone who had any influence over Johnathan's decisions. When they were finally all alone, Carla plotted and began to overspend and steal Johnathan`s hard earned money.

At a game, Johnathan injured his knee and was immediately hospitalized. Carla rushed to the hospital where the doctors told Johnathan he may never be able to play. Johnathan stayed hospitalized and Carla went back to the house, nervous that her safety net may soon be compromised. While at the house, one of Johnathan`s teammates came over to check on Johnathan. Carla immediately went into action and seduced the player with her beauty and charm.

Johnathan was released from the hospital early. He called Carla to pick him up, but she didn't answer the phone. Struggling into the house on crunches, he opened his bedroom door and found Carla in the bed with his teammate. Johnathan was devastated. He stood frozen watching the deceitful betrayal of the one whom he loved and whom he abandoned his family for. His heartbreak was unbearable.

In his sorrow, Johnathan reached out to his mother for the first time in months. To his surprise, she was already on her way to visit after hearing about his injury. The family reconciled and Johnathan's parents temporarily moved in and helped nurse him back to health. While with his parents Johnathan became very involved in the church at the advice of his mother. His dilemma caused him to seek to his "Higher Power" for help. Shortly after rekindling ties with his parents, Johnathan got the word from his doctor that he was healed and could go back to work.

Johnathan began to play with a newfound passion and zeal. He topped the national charts in his scoring. He stayed in church, and his pastor encouraged Johnathan to start a youth outreach group to help at-risk male children in his neighborhood. Johnathan felt a new sense of purpose as he mentored the youth and caused several of them to turn their lives around for the better. Johnathan even paid for several of the boys in his group to go to college.

Every free moment Johnathan had, he used it to spend time with his youth group. As time went by, Johnathan met a beautiful lady who was a mentor at his church. She often volunteered her time to help with the boys. The two ended up dating, and Johnathan decided to ask her to marry him.

Today, Johnathan has a great marriage and three beautiful children as a result of his union. He now realizes what means the most in life. Johnathan's wife helped him expand his outreach; now he has his own foundation that helps boys throughout their state.

Take notice. Things were going well for Johnathan until he got involved with Carla. Johnathan's low self-esteem caused him to make Carla his idol. He even deserted his parents for her. God had a plan for Johnathan, so he allowed him to get injured, so his eyes would open up to Carla's impure heart and motives. Johnathan's obstacle had a purpose. It led him to reconcile with his family and get rid of Carla. Then his life was restored.

Johnathan started giving back to the boys in the church, which changed his heart and gave him great compassion. God rewarded Johnathan by sending him a helper and a wife whom he shares the same purpose with. Today, Johnathan is happy because he is operating in his purpose. He now gets total fulfillment by serving God and giving back.

Now that you have seen these two examples of giving back, in what ways can you offer your service to God? Are you ready for a better life full of joy, happiness, and finally fulfillment?

If so, follow me in this acclamation! "Today, I am empowered because I know just what I must do to maintain a victorious life. Today, I commit myself to constantly searching for ways to give back to God. I will assess my talents and skill sets and constantly prepare gifts to my Creator. I now understand as I bless others, God will bless me. I will no longer look for my compensation from man. Instead, I will look to my "Higher Power," who is the One I will offer my gifts to. I will succeed because I will practice God's principles of success. I am powerful because I am a cheerful giver!"

Congratulations! You now have the formula to overcome your obstacles and maintain your success. Study these principles and apply them to your life! You will be amazed how quickly your obstacles will begin to subside!

QUESTIONS

1. Why is giving back important?
2. What is the law of reciprocity?
3. What is the difference between a gift and compensation?
4. What are the three kinds of gifts we can give to God by giving to others?
5. What is the difference between giving to individuals and giving to God?
6. What does God do to our relationships when we make people our idols?
7. Why is it against God's principles for us to have idols?

WRITING ASSIGNMENT

Study the ways we can offer service to God that are displayed in this chapter. Then create three gifts you can offer Him in each category: time, service, and money. Be specific with your answers.

IX. THE VIRTUE OF PERSISTENCE AND DETERMINATION

POINT 9:

"Despite my opposition and what others say or believe. I've got a made-up mind, no turning back. I'm determined to succeed!"

It's going to take determination to stand during the storm! In this chapter, we will discuss strategies and techniques to maintain our drive and determination. These are key weapons we can utilize when our inner strength fails. Let's study this chapter thoroughly and allow these techniques to become one with us. You will be surprised how much increased strength you will have to make it through the storm.

When obstacles occur, you need strength to make your way through them. Often people fail because they lack drive and ambition. Their lack of faith causes them to become stagnant, and they lose their will to fight. We must not allow this fate to become our portion! The only way to make it is to fight your way through!

Life's obstacles are like a big bully who tortures children at school by extorting them for their lunch money. Out of fear, most kids give in to the bully's tactics. Then there is that one child who gave in to the bully before but is tired of the constant harassment. He stands up to the bully and tells him, "You can't have my things any longer! Enough is enough!" The bully looks at the small figured child and laughs, trying to intimidate the child with his large frame and loud voice. The small child doesn't back down and rolls his fists up at the bully. The little child closes his eyes and swings with all his might! The big bully immediately falls on the floor, and instead of getting back up to fight, the bully rolls around on the floor and cries! The small, frail child opens his eyes to discover he is a champion! What he thought would be his greatest battle turned out to be one of the his greatest victories!

Just like the frail child, we have been beaten down and bruised by obstacles of life. Frightened at times by the potential consequences of our dilemmas. We flood our minds with negative thoughts. What if I fail? What if I don't make it? Some of us face our fears and push through, while others give up and quit. Quitting is not an option this time around! We are clearly aware that our fear is: **f**alse **e**vidence **a**ppearing **r**eal. We no longer fall for the same old tricks that used to keep us down! We now stand up courageously and make our way through these storms of life.

I used to be the type to wait on others to build up my confidence or boost my faith to do something. Being incarcerated away from all those I loved and admired, I had to build up the courage to move forward. It wasn't easy, but as I envisioned the goals I wanted to accomplish and I meditated on them, it boosted my desire to achieve them. In my circumstance, the walk I was about to take could only be done alone. Step one to my success was digging deep down inside and believing in me.

The key to sustaining our strength through the storm is learning how to motivate ourselves. In order to win this race and successfully overcome our tests and trials, we must become our own coach. Today is the day we will put on our coach's cap and place the whistles around our necks. Instead of waiting for others to motivate us, we will begin to motivate ourselves!

During the storms of life, we are often left alone. God purposely blocks the interference of people to force us to grow and advance through this journey on our own. There will be times when no one is there to give you a pat on your back or tell you that you can make it. Instead of relying on others, we must begin to look for strength from our "Higher Power," then rely on ourselves for encouragement.

Self-confidence is necessary to sustain during the storms of life. The enemy of our souls strategically attacks our self-esteem from childhood because he knows whatever we believe we will certainly achieve. Therefore, the enemy desperately tries to paralyze us, so we won't believe in ourselves. He then counteracts his attack by flooding us with thoughts of shame and guilt, so we won't feel worthy to succeed. And if we feel unworthy, we will give up and not fight. It is extremely important that you open your eyes to the enemy's deceptive tactics! We counter his attack by purposely building up our self-esteem and begin to rid ourselves of all feelings of unworthiness. When we are confident and believe we are in fact worthy of God's blessings and rewards, we are unstoppable! With this knowledge, we dethrone every trap the enemy has set, and we defeat Him! The enemy has no power over us! You must seal this in your mind: "I am God's wonderful creation. He made me the way I am because I am special to Him With God I can do all things. His greatest desire is to bless me. I will gladly receive all the wonderful gifts God has intended to give me. I am victorious because I know my

God loves me." We must program ourselves to receive these positive thoughts into our hearts and minds.

When troubles come our way, we must create our own report of what we will receive. We must not let anyone else dictate our outcome! Immediately, we are to say to ourselves, "Everything is going to be all right! This situation will not hurt me. I have the power within to overcome this. I can make it." This is a positive affirmation. We must intentionally create affirmations to help influence our outcome! Remember, what we believe is what we will receive. We truly control our destiny by the power of our thoughts.

To create an affirmation, first you must determine what you want your result to be. For instance, if you need to pass a test to get your degree, you know your desired result is to pass the test. You then begin to say to yourself: "I am smart. I have the ability to succeed! I will pass this test, and every other test I need to pass in life!" You take this statement and constantly feed it to yourself as if it were food. By doing this you increase your self-esteem and give yourself the inner drive to move forward and achieve your goal. As we believe in ourselves, we ultimately begin to achieve our objectives! We become unstoppable and energized, ready to jump over every hurdle in life. Success begins with confidence in "self!"

Determination is built on the basis of two main ingredients, desire and faith. As we develop these two attributes to our character, we empower ourselves. Determination is developed over a course of time. As we increase our faith and pass the test of life, our determination grows. In this season, let's take the time out to learn how to sharpen up on the characteristic of determination. When you become determined you can stand firm no matter what comes your way!

Desire is the inner passion, the need and the longing of a thing. It is desire that produces the necessary energy within us to keep us motivated. Without desire it is impossible to achieve success. In order to receive your reward after passing the test in life, you must desire to become victorious. Desire helps create the determination to move forward even when you are hurting or suffering from affliction. This power is stirred deep down inside and pushes you to dust yourself off from life's defilements and move forward to achieve success. Therefore, the intentional emotion of desire is a vital prerequisite to overcoming adversity.

Desire starts as a seed within that must be cultivated and developed. Desire is increased by constant thought. You have to want to achieve so badly that you are constantly thinking about it! Envision a time in your life when you desperately wanted something. You worked hard to achieve it, and in your spare time you often dreamed about it. Chances are you achieved your goal because your desire and inner drive helped you receive the strength to obtain it.

As our own coach, we have to develop creative ways to constantly stir up our desires. While going through a trial, it is important to visualize a successful ending. This picture should be crystal clear, just as if it were real and already our portion. As we capture and hold this photo in our minds perfectly, we become closer and closer to achieving our goal!

A good technique to help you envision your success is to create a vision board. Take a large cardboard and decorate it with magazine pictures of what you want to achieve. If you want to get married, put a picture of your wedding dress on the board. If you want a certain house, find it in a magazine and place it on your board. If you want your health back, put a picture of you happy and in good health on the board. If you need a certain amount of money, create a check and write it out to yourself for the amount you need. Whatever your desires are, captivate that picture on your visualization board. Every time you look at this board, it should make you feel happy. Stare at it and study the things affixed to the board. Tell yourself, "This is a board that represents my future life. I will have everything I want just as it appears on this board! I am successful! I will achieve!" Feed yourself with these types of thoughts daily as you view your board. Every time you undergo challenges and need a boost of energy, take out this board and repeat this process! You will be amazed with the amount of energy you'll gain from this technique! Make sure you include an image on your board that reminds you of your "Higher Power," who is the source of your success.

I used vision boards to boost my faith while incarcerated. Instead of using cardboard, I would make the cover of my notebooks vision boards. Cutting out magazines and using pictures of myself and my family, I created beautiful notebooks that I would use as writing journals. Each day I would use these notebooks to remind me of my plans. Through images I saw, and by writing my goals down daily in my journal, I boosted my desires and eventually they turned into reality! You can do the same!!

After you develop your visualization board, you will have a good picture in your mind of your desired results. You can now further increase your desire by visualizing yourself in your desired state. In your mind, create your own movie. See yourself waking up in the morning happy, living in your dream house! Look at the paintings on the wall and see how you have your house nicely decorated. Go out to the garage and jump into your dream car and go for a ride. Look at your neighborhood and wave to your friendly neighbors. Drive up to the doors of your dream job and view your co-workers. See yourself being successful in your activities at the job. End your day by going back home to your dream house to spend time with your family. Experience the love and joy you will receive from them. Feel all the feelings you will experience as if you actually received this picture as your portion! Then begin to thank your "Higher Power" for bringing it to pass. As a thanksgiving offering, see yourself preparing your gift of appreciation to your "Higher Power."

Envision yourself giving back to your Universal family. Feel the feelings of satisfaction from giving back. Lastly, see your "Higher Power" looking down on you, smiling at your wonderful achievements.

Remember, during your obstacles the enemy will constantly try and bombard your mind with negative thoughts. His goal is to mentally and emotionally imprison you by getting you to accept his illusions as factual. We counteract the enemy's attack by dismantling those negative thoughts and feeding our minds with positive thoughts. These thoughts are produced when we say affirmations and believe them, and when we go into meditation and produce positive visualization in our minds.

Just as we need physical food to survive, we need inspirational thoughts to maintain through the storms of life. Just as a car cannot run without gas, we will collapse if we don't fill our minds with positive thoughts. It is important that each day we take the time we need to coach ourselves. This self-motivation when built properly, is the key ingredient that will keep us standing when others fold. We must watch what we allow our minds to eat, especially during the storm! When we eat correctly by feeding ourselves positive thoughts, we will begin to soar through life!

In addition to desire, we need faith. Desire is a longing for a thing. Faith is the belief you can obtain it. Desire without faith is useless! Many of us long for things, but we will never achieve them, because we don't believe we can have them. It is our faith that makes our desires become reality. We need faith to overcome the storm! When desire is mixed with faith it creates the most powerful vibration to the subconscious mind, which translates into prayer to our "Higher Power." It is our faith in our prayers being answered that produces miraculous results! When you believe you can achieve your desire, it will come to pass.

God is impressed with those who have faith in Him. We have learned through our past failures that we need our "Higher Power" in order to sustain. As we develop our partnership with Him, we are able to see our newfound strength and power. As we begin to recognize and believe we can do all things with Him, we develop faith that produces results!

Faith is developed as we learn about and trust in the abilities of our "Higher Power." Our greatest faith is developed as we read and study our Holy Book. The stories in this book are inspired by God to specifically increase our faith! When times are rough and our faith is shaken, the best thing we can do is pick up and read our Holy Book. As we read the stories in the book, our faith immediately is strengthened. We begin to realize we are not in this battle by ourselves, but we have our "Higher Power" with us at all times. This inner assurance gives us faith to pick ourselves up and move forward!

Another great way of increasing our faith is by reading inspirational books that encourage us. Just as your spirit has been strengthened by reading this book, you can continuously feed yourself with good inspirational food from other books. As important as it is to pick up a bite to eat to maintain your strength, make reading inspirational books a part of your life as well! If you do, you will always have the spiritual food you need to inspire, encourage, and uplift you. Any time you are experiencing difficulties, you can read your inspirational books that will strengthen your spirit and help you continue on your journey. Make reading inspirational books a habit in your life. If you do, you will sustain the determination that you need to succeed!

Inspirational books also include autobiographies and testimonies of others who have endured the same obstacles as you have. You can read their experiences and learn from the strategies they used to overcome. As they succeed in the story line, your faith strengthens because you too share in that moment through reading. You see that they are just like you! Just as they overcame, you too can overcome! Go to the bookstore or library and find some books about people who you admire. Read them and discover the common pattern of success.

Time in prayer is essential to maintaining stability. Without it, it is almost impossible to be successful. As we learn to develop a relationship with our "Higher Power," we can trust and gain an inner assurance that everything is going to be all right. We know we can go to Him at any time, at any place, and ask for help. We gain an assurance that He hears us and will quickly respond to our request. This assurance helps increase our faith! The more time we spend with God and utilize prayer, the more we are able to see just how wonderful and faithful God is! Time and experience with God are two key factors that help increase our faith. Remember, you will have not, if you ask not! Therefore, open your mouth and let your request be made known unto God!

Now that we have explored the key factors to increasing our determination, it is time to apply these techniques to our lives. As they become one with us, we will begin to automatically use them and increase our mental strength!

We previously learned that whatever behavior we do repeatedly over a course of two to three weeks, it becomes a habit. In order to overcome the storms of life, we must create and develop a schedule so we can consciously implement these techniques into our lives.

As we discussed in an earlier chapter, our mornings are very important! The way we start our day is the way we will finish it! Therefore, it is important to get off to a good start! Before you open your eyes in the morning, meditate and take control of your day! Thank God for allowing you to see another day and ask Him to let his presence surround you and protect you from evil. Then coach yourself by utilizing your affirmations.

After you successfully complete these techniques, you are free to start your day. As you brush your teeth, look in the mirror and speak to yourself. For example, say, "'Self,' you are beautiful. I love you very much. 'Self,' you are special to me and you are special to God. I will do everything in my power to protect you and keep you from harm. Before I make any decisions, I'll always keep your best interest in mind. You are a priority to me, and I will treat you like the awesome person that you are. 'Self,' you are my hero." Say these types of affirmations and mean what you say! As you do so, you will begin to feel good about "self!"

Before you go outside, read a passage from your Holy Book and/or daily meditation. Take the time to ponder on the positive thoughts in that passage and clear out all negative thoughts and energy from your mind. Believe in your heart your day will be successful, and you are sure to achieve your goal!

As you drive to work, pop in an inspirational recording. Fill your being with the positive thoughts and allow that message to reflect in your heart.

Carry a bag with you at all times with some form of inspirational reading material. Read it during your breaks or your lunch hour.

Before you go to sleep at night, close your eyes and meditate. Review your experiences throughout the day. Congratulate yourself for your victories, then replay the events you would like to see work out differently. Review these events in your mind, and then replay them as you would like to see them occur. Repeat some positive affirmations in your mind, and then peacefully go to sleep.

As you make these practices a part of your daily routine, you will soar to heights that you never dreamed was possible! Becoming successful is a process that takes work. It is up to each of us to develop a disciplined system that leads us onto the path of victory. We develop this system by making healthy habits become a part of our lifestyle. There is no doubt that we will endure many obstacles, trials, and/or tribulations. We now understand these situations aren't sent to destroy us, but they are meant to lead us on the right track, build us up and make us strong!

We no longer have to feel discouraged or hopeless. We now possess the knowledge of how to stare our obstacles in the face, take up our inner courage, and push through these hurdles of life.

Are you ready to become victorious and develop your inner ambition and drive to succeed?

Well, follow me in reciting this positive affirmation: "Today, I have the power to achieve every one of my dreams and goals. I will no longer accept the negative reports of what others say or believe.

"Today, I know I can make it, so I'm determined to succeed! Each day I will work on helping develop my faith and desire by saying positive affirmations daily, practicing visualization, and by praying and reading inspirational material. Whenever I'm down, I will get up! I will not let bad news get the best of me. I will take control over my destiny by creating my own report of my desired outcome.

"Daily, I will visualize my success. I will yearn for it constantly by focusing my thoughts on seeing my victory. I will stir up my faith and believe until I see my success come to pass! I am victorious today because I am empowered! Despite my opposition and what others say or believe, my mind is made up and I'm not turning back. I am determined to succeed!"

QUESTIONS

1. Why is determination a key characteristic needed to overcome?
2. Why is it important that we become our own coach?
3. Why is self-confidence a key factor in obtaining success?
4. What are affirmations? Why are they useful?
5. What's the difference between faith and desire?
6. What is a visualization board? Why is it an effective tool?
7. How do you create your own visualization movie in your mind?

WRITING ASSIGNMENT

Write out your daily schedule for increasing your determination. Record just what techniques you will implement and at what times you will practice each technique daily. Follow this schedule closely and watch how effective the results will be.

X. SOLUTION FOCUSED!

POINT 10:

"My focus is my focus and my focus doesn't change. There is nothing you can do to make my focus rearrange."

In order to push through the billows of life and overcome our obstacles, we must learn how to focus on the solution, rather than the problem. Many of us are great starters. We begin ventures with lots of strength and determination. However, midway through, our energy decreases and we slack off in our efforts. Some of us never make it to the end. We quit and give up, instead of fighting our way through. It is important that we maintain our enthusiasm and determination as we discussed in the previous chapter. It is also essential that we concentrate on the resolution to our dilemmas. It's time to get focused!

In this chapter, we will learn how to stay solution focused throughout our obstacles, empowering ourselves with key strategies that will help us cross over the finish line and overcome our hurdles. Study these techniques and implement them! You will be amazed how much your focus will intensely increase!

The enemy studies us from birth. He knows our likes and dislikes, as well as our weaknesses. He strategically equips those who he assigns to our lives to play on our vulnerabilities. His hope is that we will be naïve and fall for his trap by accepting these people into our lives. Don't fall for the bait!

When someone is in our lives who is on assignment from the enemy, God sends obstacles our way to warn us that we have gone off course. If we do not get rid of these people, the obstacles God sends intensifies! God turns up the heat to reveal to us the heart and intent of these people. They begin to show their hand, which signals us that the person does not have our best interest at heart. Many of us see the signs, yet our insecurities and our fear of loneliness keeps us from doing what we know we should do, - detach! If you stay in a relationship with someone who is on assignment by the enemy to destroy your life, they will ultimately cause you to self-destruct! These people drain our energy and distract us from taking care of "self." It is very important that you stop and open your eyes to see those who are assigned to destroy you!

The enemy's major goal is to distract us. If he can keep our minds consumed on meaningless things, we will be derailed from taking care of the important things that help us reach our purpose. In this chapter, we will discuss the characteristics of focus and its attributes. As we learn how to properly focus our attention, we will begin to close the door to the enemy and his tactics. As we embrace the power of focus, nothing will be impossible for us to achieve!

Focus is a concentrated effort of mental energy that is used to accomplish a task. It is the determination to concentrate on a thing until it comes to pass. Proper focus keeps us from becoming sidetracked or distracted.

If we do not properly handle our obstacles, we can easily be distracted by them. Obstacles often cause us to be overwhelmed by negative thoughts of worry, fear, or doubt. These negative motions cam consume our time and require a lot of energy. Negative thoughts do not produce any positive results! It is the enemy's desire that we utilize our time consuming ourselves with negative thoughts so that we will not be productive. We cannot allow ourselves to fall into his traps! Therefore, when problems arise, we are to purposely change our perception and figure out what we can do to change our course. When we resist thinking negatively by refocusing our minds with positive thoughts, we position ourselves to win the battle!

A large part of overcoming our obstacles begins and ends within the mind. The mind, in essence, is our battlefield. Whatever we believe, we will ultimately receive! As we learn how to take control of our minds, we position ourselves to win whatever battle or obstacle that comes our way! As we master the techniques in the book, we will become empowered to mentally destroy whatever storms we endure. Learning to control our thoughts is not an easy thing. It takes discipline and constant practice. There will be many times that we fail to contain our thoughts. Don't beat yourself up! Learn from your lesson and immediately put these techniques back into practice!

Some people have been sent in our lives by the enemy to distract us from working on "self." These people intrude on our emotions by pushing their own agendas. We find ourselves neglecting "self" to help them accomplish their own goals. It is important that we do not let people deter us from our mission!

Distractions also include televisions, cell phones, and telephones. Oftentimes, these things will take us off course from accomplishing our mission. The first step to establishing focus is by uncovering the areas and things that distract us the most. When we identify our distractions, we must immediately dissemble them! Do not allow distractions to remain a part of your life. If you do, it will delay you from reaching your destination and can eventually destroy you!

The best way to stay focused is to create a concrete plan of solution. Nothing can be accomplished without a plan. Our plan of solution will become our detailed written road map that provides us with directions on how we will get where we need to go. This plan will require concentrated thought. We have been utilizing our minds throughout this journey to help us overcome our dilemmas. We learned how to go into meditation and seek out our "Higher Power" for instructions. We learned what things we need to do and how to work on and care for "self." Now it is time to put all this information together, creating our own solution book. When we create this book and follow the plans within it, it will help us to stay focused and avoid things which don't promote our mission. Once we commit to our solution book plan, we set the boundaries for our lives in this season. If we follow this plan, we are sure to see drastic improvements, which will help us overcome our obstacles.

It is common theory to think we can just plan in our minds and don't need to write down our plan. This theory is incorrect! A real plan needs to include strategy. It is hard to create a strategy without visually determining what you may be up against. When you are able to put your plan on paper, you are forced to think and possibly expand on your ideas and strategies. A good plan details costs and hidden factors that you may not have anticipated. It also provides alternatives. If plan A doesn't work, I can still accomplish my mission by changing to plan B. In essence, our plan helps us to strategize our approach!

Most successful people are strategists. They prepare themselves for unseen difficulties so they will be able to stand regardless of the obstacles they endure. We must do the same by creating an organized plan that includes the steps we need to take to get from where we presently are, to where we need to go. In the next section of this chapter we will learn step by step, how to create our own personal "Solution Book." If you take heed to the instructions and follow the plan you implemented, your dilemma will be much easier to overcome!

The *first step* in creating your Solution Book is to create a cover page. On the center of a blank page label your page, "My Solution Book," in bold, big, upper case letters. Skip a few lines down and write, "Created by," and insert your name.

On the next sheet of paper, you will move on to *step two* by drafting your objective. Write out the word "Objective" and underline it. Put a hyphen next to the word. Your objective is to overcome your obstacle. For example, if you are currently enduring a financial hardship, your objective could be, "I will overcome my current financial problems." Whatever your problem is, state it in your objective and also state that you will overcome it.

Step three will consist of writing your mission statement. On the next line under your objective, write: "Mission Statement." Underline it just as you did your objective. Then place a hyphen next to it and write out your mission statement. A mission statement is the main strategy you will use to overcome your dilemma. For example, if your problems require you to seek help or do research, your mission statement could be: "I will overcome my dilemma by committing to researching available options that will bring me into enlightenment and help me solve my problem." If your problem requires you to work on and change "self," your mission statement could be: "I will commit to working on "self" daily, until I rid myself of all known character defects. As I change "self," I will overcome my dilemmas."

Whatever the main issue is, write out how you will fix this issue. Your mission statement is the very thing you need to change that will help you overcome your obstacle. In many cases your mission may be to simply change your mindset and your perception about your dilemma, so that you can stand strong during the storm. In this case, your mission statement could be: "I will learn how to effectively take control of my thoughts. I will change my perspective and view my dilemma for what it truly is - an opportunity to make me a better "self." Take time out and think about what you want to gain out of this experience. Whatever your main goal should become your mission statement.

The *fourth step* is to create our strategy. In order to achieve our mission, we must implement several techniques within our strategy. We will number each one of them, so we can clearly detail the steps we will take to accomplish our mission.

Directly under your "Mission Statement," write the section "Strategy." Underline it and put a hyphen next to it.

Underneath strategy, label it #1 and start with your first strategy to overcome your obstacles. As we learned in this book, the first thing we must do to stand during our storm is change our perspective. We cannot view the storm as a bad thing; we must see it as an opportunity to become a greater "self." Point 1 should include changing our perspective. For example, you could say in Point 1: "In order to get through this obstacle, I must change my perspective. I will do this by purposely seeing the good that will come from this situation. I believe this obstacle will not hurt me, but it will make me stronger by causing me to eliminate negative people and things out of my life and causing me to work on "self.""

In ***Point 1*** make sure you include what you will do to change your perspective. Also include what good things will come out of this situation.

Point 2 will show how you will utilize your "Higher Power" to get you through the storm. For example, "I will make it through my dilemma by creating a partnership with my "Higher Power." I know with Him all things are possible."

You can also include sub points to detail more strategies you will use for each point. For example, underneath Point 2 you can list:

A – I will spend at least fifteen minutes each day in prayer to my Higher Power.

B – I will read my Holy Book every morning.

You can input as many sub points as you wish to detail your strategy.

Point 3 will include how you will utilize meditation to keep you calm during the storm. For example, when trouble arises, I will not react adversely to it; instead, I will stop and change my course by meditating.

Your sub points for Point 3, could include:

A – I will meditate in the morning before I open my eyes."

B – I will meditate and recap my day before I close my eyes."

C – Throughout the day I will see myself whole and reaching each goal that I set.

Make your strategy personal and specific! This is the road map you will use to help you overcome your obstacle. When you are challenged, you need to utilize it to find the strategy to pick you back up.

Point 4 will include how you will constantly dismantle shame and guilt out of your life, after you properly deal with the purpose behind these emotions. For example, "I will not let shame and guilt settle within me. If I feel guilty for doing something, I will address my guilt by taking responsibility for my actions. Then I will free myself of this emotion. When I get rid of guilt, shame will no longer be allowed to set in."

Some sub points for Point 4 can include:

A – I will examine myself daily to make sure I don't have any feelings of shame and guilt.

B – I will monitor my actions and not allow myself to do things I will later regret.

Point 5 will include the things you can actively do to overcome your obstacle. List the main thing you must do first, and then list all other actions in your sub points. For example, "I will no longer stay stagnant in my troubles. I will always make an assessment of what I can actively do to overcome my dilemma. As I work on "self," my circumstances will change.

Sub points to Point 5 could be:

A – I will go back to school and further my education.

B – I will go to counseling.

Point 5 will probably be one of your largest in context; it is the detailed things you know you must do to overcome your hurdle. Write out your sub points in detail. Be very specific!

Point 6 will include the strategies you can use to begin to care for "self." For example, "I will make me a priority and learn to care for self."

The sub points to Point 6 for examples can include:

A – I will learn how to love myself.

B – I will learn how to create boundaries.

Be aware that Point 6 is going to be another large point. Be specific and go into detail of what you will do to care for "self."

Point 7 will include the strategies you will use to find your purpose. For example, "I will no longer live a dull, empty, pointless life. I will discover my purpose!"

Sub points for Point 7 can include:

A – I will take time to discover my skill sets and talents.

B – I will analyze the environments I'm most comfortable in.

Utilize your notes and go back and read chapter 7 so you can figure out what you can do to get closer to discovering your purpose.

Point 8 includes strategies you will implement to give back. For example, "I will soar in life by learning effective ways to give back."

Sub points of Point 8 can include:

A – I will give my gift of money to my local church.

B – I will give my gift of time to the local nursing home.

Be specific in your points so you can implement the service of giving back into your life!

Point 9 includes strategies you can use to increase and sustain your determination. For example, "No matter what comes my way, I will sustain. I won't give up no matter the cost. I am determined to succeed."

Sub points for Point 9 can include:

A – Daily, I will look at my vision board.

B – Before I open my eyes in the morning, I will visualize myself achieving victory.

Point 10 includes strategies you will implement to help you keep your focus. For example, "I will no longer concentrate on my problem, instead I must focus on the solution."

Sub points for Point 10 can include:

A – I will study my Solution Book daily.

B – I will eliminate people who are distractions to me.

Just as you are specific in all the other points, be specific in the strategies you will use to stay focused.

After you create your Solution Book, honor it and keep it with you at all times! When times get rough you can review it and be strengthened by your own positive words.

You can change your Solution Book as often as you need to. As we write we begin to internalize the information that we are taking in. The more you write out your strategies, the more they will become one with you!

As you implement your plan, new strategies may arise. In this case, you need to go back to the drawing board. Constantly change your plan as you change! You will gain fulfillment as you continue to improve "self" by accomplishing your goals. Your solution book will assist you with keeping track of your progress. It can be an excellent instrument that can help you grow and keep your excited about your mission.

The less you look at your problems and focus on your solution, the more you will become empowered! Focusing on the solution will force it to become your portion! Instead of becoming frightened and stagnant, you will be driven to make it through the storm and overcome!

Your Solution Book is a key part of your success. Many times, even though we know what to do, we forget or neglect to do it! By focusing on the strategies in our Solution Book, we are constantly reminding ourselves in a positive way, of our abilities and our need to overcome.

Don't just read this chapter; get active by creating your Solution Book! Refuse to let life dictate your provisions and destiny! Take charge of your life by putting together your detailed plan of what you can do. As you began to act on the strategies that are included in your plan, you will begin to feel good about "self." Your self-esteem will also increase as you become proud of your accomplishments. Don't just sit on this information. Act! Start your Solution Book today! You will be amazed by the results!

Are you ready to channel your focus on the solution? If so, follow me in this affirmation of focus. "Today, I am empowered. Today, I have control over my focus. I will no longer be sidetracked by traps sent by the enemy. I will rid myself of all people, places, and things that keep me from achieving my purpose.

I will work hard in creating my Solution Book. I will create a specific detailed plan of how I will overcome and improve "self." I will look at this plan daily and do whatever it takes to accomplish my goals. I am no longer helpless and weak. I am strengthened with the wisdom and knowledge I need to stand strong during this storm. Today I am an overcomer! I know that I will make it! I am built to outlast this storm!"

Congratulations! You have taken a huge step in your pursuit to overcoming life's obstacles! Your Solution Book will be your road map that will lead you out of the storm! See you on the other side of this journey in your divine destination called victory!

QUESTIONS

1. Why is it important to learn how to focus?
2. Where does our biggest battle take place?
3. In which ways does the enemy try to keep us distracted?
4. What happens if we don't detach from people who are on assignment by the enemy?
5. Name three major devices that are distractions to people?
6. Why is creating a plan necessary for goal achievement?
7. What is an objective, a mission statement, and a strategy?

WRITING ASSIGNMENT

Create your Solution Book. Detail each point and be specific.

XI. ENJOYING THE JOURNEY OF LIFE

POINT 11:

"If I purposely rid myself of all anger, worry, and strife. I'll learn to embrace each day, enjoying this journey of life."

For many years I was one of those type of people that no matter how much I had, the void inside me had me seeking for more. Consequently, I never got to really enjoy the journey of life, I just experienced it. Oddly, it was my time behind bars that I was able to consciously enjoy my daily experiences as I honestly measured my growth. This made me realize that even in dark spaces of our lives, we can still position ourselves to enjoy the journey. Don't get me wrong, every day will not be a great day. However, we can look for the good in each day and purposely experience it!

Many of us have become overwhelmed by the various trials and tribulations we have endured in life. Filled with anger and frustration and confused by life's mishaps, we begin to dread each day rather than embracing it with joy. Life is God's wonderful gift to each of us. Tests and trials are not sent to keep us down, they are meant to strengthen us and to encourage our growth. It is very important that we view life's obstacles correctly so that our spirits can become at ease. Instead of dreading our experiences, we should embrace them with joy!

Each obstacle brings us closer to fulfillment and purpose. There is so much to learn from each experience we endure. Instead of becoming frustrated and trying to quickly escape the route of our test, we must learn how to relax and enjoy the beauty of each experience. *Remember*, there is no way to get through an obstacle, except to go through! We cannot advance to our next level of life, until we pass each test. Therefore, there is no use in trying to run from our dilemmas or attempt to avoid them. Instead, we must stand up with courage and face every obstacle that comes our way! God will provide us with the strength and wisdom to overcome each dilemma once we seek Him for guidance. We are not in this battle alone; we have our Partner for support. With our Partner, we can overcome any obstacle that comes our way. With Him, we will pass all of our tests with flying colors!

Knowing that we will ultimately get the victory, we can relax! This experience doesn't have to be that difficult. We can change our experience by changing how we view it. If we see it as hard and difficult to overcome, it will be that way! If we see it as enjoyable and easy to conquer, it will be that way! Our experience is within our own control! It is up to us to set the stage of what we will allow ourselves to believe.

In this chapter, we will learn how to enjoy life, despite our obstacles and dilemmas. We will learn how to change our perception of our experiences, embrace them and enjoy their significance. Once we embrace these methods for living an enjoyable life, we will ultimately become empowered to endure any season or difficulty life may bring.

Life is created to be pleasurable. We were all uniquely designed to enjoy the experiences we will encounter on earth. Man was created with five senses—the ability to see, hear, smell, touch, and taste. God gave us these abilities to appreciate life here on earth!

Regardless of what we endure, life can be fun! When we know tests are sent to develop us and make us strong, we can embrace them by purposely looking for the good that can come out of them. We must not allow ourselves to accept the enemy's bait of depression. It is impossible to enjoy life while experiencing negative emotions! Instead, we are to look for the good within each day and make the best out of all of our situations. This is the way that we will become victorious. When we fall, we wipe ourselves off, learn from our mistakes, and then quickly begin again. We do not wallow in our sorrow. We accept our temporary failures as part of our many life experiences that we can learn from.

Life is comparable to a game of bowling that we play with our friends. Sometimes, we will get a strike and knock down all the pins. Other times, we will not. The more we practice, the better we develop our skills. If we throw a gutter ball, we do not fall down in the bowling alley and kick and scream.

We say, "Oh, man!" And even laugh at our mistake, then pick up the ball to try again. We observe others around us and learn from their skill and precision. We closely watch and improve our technique. We don't dread the experience. We actually enjoy it! As a result, the game becomes entertaining to us. We love it even more as we master our technique. This should be the same way we enjoy life! We must learn to accept the good along with the bad. We take the good and master it to become better, and we take the bad and find the good in it. We learn to be content in whatever state we are in by learning how to label all our experiences as good, no matter what they are. For example, if you lose your job, you don't cry and give up. You go to your Partner and ask for guidance. You work on solving your problem, but in the meantime, you learn to take advantage of your free time at home. Enjoy your temporary vacation and enjoy the lessons you acquired from your dilemma. When you know how to counterattack your obstacles properly, they no longer become obstacles, they become opportunities for advancement!

During the rough times of life, we are not to look at our obstacles, but we are to look for opportunities of advancement and enjoy them! Instead of fighting against our experiences, we yield to the good that lies within them. Then we ride it straight home to the finish line! As we do, life no longer becomes displeasing, it becomes fun.

Think about little children. You can put them on punishment, send them to their rooms, and take away their toys and their television. If you peep in the room thirty minutes later, you will observe the child making spaceships out of his books and action figures out of his pencils. You tried to punish the child, yet he is still having fun. Why? Children are programmed to look for the fun in every situation. Their minds haven't yet been contaminated. They have not been beaten down by life's obstacles. We must re-program our minds to become liken to those little children, and purposely relish every experience we undergo. We do that by looking for ways we can enjoy ourselves, regardless of our outward circumstances.

We enjoy life by waking up each day with an attitude of gratitude. We do this by thinking about all the wonderful things we have to be grateful for, and we give God thanks for them. As we recount all that we have been blessed with, our hearts fill with joy. When we become grateful, our spirits in turn becomes full of praise and thanksgiving. It's like getting good news no matter what's happening in life. If we get a call that we won the lottery, we instantly become happy and zealous. By having an attitude of gratitude, recounting good memories and good times, we can automatically create the same type of inner joy. When we are happy, we look for more happy experiences. Instead of seeking out the bad, we look for the good. Whatever we seek is essentially what we will get!

Make up your mind today to enjoy life. Live each day as if it were your last, by getting the most out of the experience. Don't allow obstacles to beat you down. Conquer them and allow them to strengthen you! Figure out ways you can relax and enjoy yourself, even while the storm is raging. As you relax, you will see how quickly time flies, and how soon your dilemma will be over.

As I shared with you previously, imprisonment was the worst thing I could ever imagine would happen to me. For the first couple of months I was very depressed and withdrawn. One day while watching an inspirational program on the prison television, I decided to get up and make the best out of my experience. Instead of viewing jail as a dungeon, I changed my view and made it a vacation. I began to rest and use meditation to take me out of the prison whenever I wanted to leave. During my free time I would read and study for hours, purposely enjoying myself. I would also take walks around the track and field and begin to spend time with God. I learned how to take care of "self." I became my own best friend. I encourage myself when I was down, and I kept my eyes on the ending picture - freedom! Then I learned to write, and I began to enjoy my new talent. I got lost in time, spending hours writing, which also took me to another place. Instead of weeping over my misfortunes, I thought about how the experience would make me better. I concentrated on my release and the things I would do to make up for lost time. As a result of my actions, my unbearable experience became bearable and I found purpose in it! I realized my pain would not go unmerited, but it would help someone else who may be ready to give up. My success could help them gain the desire to begin again. I made a concentrated decision to stop viewing life from my own perspective, and I started to become more open minded. This change helped me gain the strength I needed to outlast my storm!

In order to get through the storm, you cannot be afraid of it, or the displeasure it may potentially bring. Go in your lab during meditation and stir up your inner joy. Be determined to overcome and enjoy the experience in doing so. As you work on this technique, you will build up your inner strength.

Even as we go through life without adversity, we tend to not enjoy ourselves. We are so busy working hard to get to another level, that we miss out on the fun within our experiences. We say to one's self, we will have fun when we retire, or when we receive this accomplishment, only to get there and still not be satisfied. The only way to truly enjoy life is to learn to purposely enjoy each experience, both good and bad. Each day should be allotted time for enjoyment. The question becomes: "What do you like to do that you find enjoyable?" As you make this discovery, implement these activities into your daily plans.

One of our most precious relationships on earth is with our family members. God purposely positioned us to be born into chosen families. It is His intent that we enjoy our family life! No matter how busy our schedules become, we must take the time to spend with our family. Friends will often come and go, but our families will forever be our relatives. Find activities that your family enjoys participating in and purposely enjoy life with your family. Eat together, go to outings together, watch movies together, and spend time sharing experiences together. Let each of your family members feel your love. Teach each other how to love the way God intended. You will find that one of the greatest experiences in life is enjoying family love.

There are many creations on earth that are built for our entertainment. It is up to us to take advantage of these places. Many people have fun by going to the movies, enjoying sporting events, frequenting restaurants, participating in charity functions and vacationing and traveling. These things were created to help us enjoy life. Take advantage of these places and allow yourself to be entertained.

Each of us have hobbies, which are things we enjoy doing in our free time. It is imperative to find hobbies that interest us and make time to do them. As we begin to enjoy doing the things we like, we improve our quality of life. Balance your life by making time to do the things you enjoy doing.

In this book, we talked about working in our areas of purpose. As we tap into and discover these areas, we will begin to enjoy our time working in them. When we are working in our purpose, time flies. We become fulfilled inside because we are doing just what God created us to do! When we discover purpose and work in it, we change our quality of life. Life no longer becomes dreadful, it becomes fun!

We discussed taking care of "self" in detail in this book. Taking care of "self" requires having fun and enjoying life. We become conscious of our own needs and begin to improve "self." As we learn how to work on "self" we should make it a fun activity. Constantly reward yourself by doing the things that makes you happy! Purpose in your mind to live well, eat well, and have a good time. As the heart becomes merry, so does the body.

Many people become infected with diseases and ailments mainly because of irregular emotions. When we allow ourselves to become filled with negative emotions such as fear, worry, anger, un-forgiveness, bitterness, and depression, we are working against God's purpose and design for our lives. As a result, our bodies malfunction. Our bodies were not created to carry negative energy. In order to enjoy good health, we must rid ourselves of all negative emotions. You will be surprised how simply changing your moods can help improve your health! The happier and more vibrant you become, the stronger your body will build up. When your body is strong it will help fight off all impurities within it.

The key to revitalizing your health is learning how to intentionally feed yourself with positive thoughts and rid yourself of all negativity. A broken heart can kill you! A happy heart will make you strong and merry! You will become empowered as you learn to implement the techniques in this book and eliminate all negativity from your life. As the negativity goes, you will see an amazing change in your quality of life changes. Therefore, live life victoriously, by purposely being merry!

Many of us have gotten disappointed in life because of the things we don't have. This is because we haven't learned how to be grateful and care for what we already have. We despise what we have so we neglect it, and in the process of doing so, we close the doors to receiving more. The way we break the cycle is to purposely become grateful for the things you do have. Honor them and care for them, and God will bring you more. When we have a heart of thanksgiving, we allow ourselves to find peace and enjoyment in any long-term circumstance we encounter. By doing this we open the doors to usher in more good experiences. The key to a joyous life is perception. Stop looking at what you do not have and get caught up in what you do have. Relax and enjoy your journey. Don't be concerned with the journey of others. Learn from experiences and work on improving "self." As you work on "self," your path will broaden, allowing you to experience great things in life! In order to sustain, we must make a conscious effort not to complain! As we become grateful, life rewards us by becoming enjoyable!

When we learn to take control of the way we view events, we become empowered. The things that used to adversely affect us and knock us out, no longer bother us. Instead of letting our situations control us, we control them by deciding how we will allow ourselves to perceive them. No longer are we pushed and shoved around in life by our emotions.

Now we can jump over every hurdle that life brings us! We become more than conquerors in all that we do! Victorious living begins with "self" control and our ability to change our perception.

In this chapter, we learned some essential key elements to purposely enjoying life. Now we will explore some examples of how we can implement these techniques to enjoy a better quality of life.

Example: Tim and Sara met in college and decided to get married. Tim worked hard to become a lawyer, and he successfully obtained his goal. Tim worked even harder to land the position of partner at a very prestigious law firm. It was his dream as a little boy, and he finally managed to achieve it! Tim and Sara bought a beautiful house, and they lived a luxurious lifestyle. Tim spent many hours in the office to sustain his income. He no longer had time for Sara and his children. Instead, he consumed himself with gaining promotions and prestige as a lawyer. As a result, Tim's marriage became rocky. Sara felt neglected and unappreciated. Tim also neglected his health, forcing his body to work under stressful conditions.

One day Sara had had enough. She decided she wanted a divorce and she went to Tim with her request. Tim, determined to sustain his ranking as a prestigious lawyer, opted to keep his profession and let Sara go. Although saddened by the circumstances, Sara made preparations to split, but suddenly Tim got ill.

Tim was rushed to the hospital where he was diagnosed with cancer. In the split second of a moment, Tim began to change his perspective. Sara came to the hospital and learned about Tim's shocking diagnosis and wept. The two cried in each other's arms.

For a month, Tim stayed in the hospital and Sara helped nurse him back to health. The two began to talk night and day, remembering the good old times. As Tim recounted the enjoyable moments, his heart was strengthened. One day he received a visit from John, his partner at the law firm. Instead of John being sympathetic about Tim's condition, he pressed Tim to hurry and get well to get back to his duties at the office. This behavior shocked Tim; he suddenly realized John did not care about him. He only cared about the work he could do.

Two weeks after Tim's hospitalization, he received a certified letter from John that demanded that he give up his position and a new partner would replace him. Tim was outraged! After all the long hours and hard work that he put in the firm, they were willing to let him go because of the seriousness of his illness and the likelihood of his non-performance.

Tim came home from the hospital a month later but was still on bed rest. Sara took a leave of absence from her job and catered to Tim. Once again, he fell in love with his wife and began to cherish her. He became so engrossed with Sara and his kids and truly enjoyed their company. The quality time together caused the family to unite. They enjoyed family night, watching movies together. And, even fellowshipped during family prayer. Their request was that God turn their situation around.

Eventually, Tim received another letter from his job, terminating his employment. Instead of crying about his dilemma, he sought God for direction and guidance. Tim and Sara had a substantial amount in savings, so the two began to think about their destinies and how they could sustain their lifestyles with Tim being sick. Tim helped Sara start her own accounting firm from home, which had always been Sara's dream.

Tim began to rejuvenate his body and each day he got better and better. After about a year, Tim had totally regained his strength. Because he appreciated and loved the time he spent with his family, he decided to also work from home. Tim used his skill set as a lawyer to defend victims of malpractice. He became very compassionate about others who were taken advantage of, as he strongly related. As a result, his passion produced results. He quickly rose to the top of his field of law and even surpassed the heights of his old law firm!

Today, Tim and Sara are still happily married. Tim vowed to never again miss the opportunity to acknowledge what is important in life. Today his cancer is in remission. He is very strong and healthy, and Tim is living a meaningful, purpose driven life!

Tim's obstacle was sent to open his eyes about what he should and should not value. His illness was not meant to kill him, it was allowed to make him a better person. He almost lost his marriage to an awesome woman because of his idol, which was accolades from colleagues and prestige. Tim's sickness helped him see how quickly he would be disregarded, if his life was suddenly over. This opened Tim's eyes to the importance of enjoying life and family.

Tim did not sit around and complain. Instead, he used his time to create a better relationship with his wife and kids. He also got busy figuring out how he could assist his family in the event that something happened to him. In turn, he helped his wife, whom he previously neglected, fulfill her dream of owning her own accounting firm. The family worked together as a team, and Tim overcame his obstacle of sickness. Tim and Sara are no different than you and I. We, too, can stand and overcome our storm!

Are you ready to purposely enjoy every experience you endure in life? Are you ready to live the abundant life God promised us? If so, follow me in this prayer for an abundant life.

"God, I thank You that You have opened my eyes and revealed the power I possess. I now take hold of this power, and I decree that I will begin to enjoy life! Each day I wake up, I will purposely look for the good that the day offers. I refuse to respond to negative emotions. Instead, I will rid myself of them by changing my perspective. I will view each circumstance as an opportunity for advancement and growth.

Therefore, I will be glad and rejoice in my day, regardless of what comes my way. When I fall short, open my eyes and help me to always see the good You have in store for me. Help me to work through every adverse circumstance and make the best out of it! Equip me with Your wisdom and knowledge and help me to grow! I thank You now for touching my heart and changing my mindset to view life from Your perspective. I now receive the abundant life that You have promised. Amen."

Congratulations! Once again you have added another weapon under your belt! Joy and happiness can help you overcome any dart or arrow that is sent your way. You are empowered to conquer! You are now positioned to overcome!

QUESTIONS

1. Why is it important to enjoy the journey of life?
2. How do we control our experiences mentally?
3. In what ways can we purposely enjoy life?
4. Why is it that little children enjoy life, no matter what happens?
5. What places were created to entertain us and help us enjoy life?
6. How does negative emotions effect our body?
7. Why is our perspective important in our pursuit to having a God life?

WRITING ASSIGNMENT

In what ways can you personally begin to enjoy life more? What will you do to make sure each day of life is pleasurable? Answer these questions and create Point 11 in your Solution Book.

XII. PERFECT PRACTICE

POINT 12:

"Now that I have a plan, I know that I won't fail! I'll practice every point, until I have them nailed!"

The key to success in life is experience. As we practice pushing through our obstacles, we learn to become experts in the field of overcoming. Our success will not occur overnight! It will take time and practice. When we fall short and fail to achieve success, we are not to label our experience as a failure. We are to look at it for what it is, simply practiced success!

I outlined in this book my mindset shift and the tools I used to overcome adversity. It must be said that this became a lifestyle for me. Practicing these points daily were my survival tools that helped me to come out on top. Even after my incarceration, I use them daily. This allows me to see the treasures in life, when others can only see the pain. You, too, can position yourself to be a master overcomer, but it is going to take some work!

Anything worth sustaining in life will come as a result of practice! It is up to each of us to intake these points, internalize them, and let them become one with us. As you do, you will find it easier to move more smoothly through life!

In this chapter, we will discuss the techniques we can use to practice each point. If you follow the directions given, you are sure to recognize a drastic improvement in your current experience.

I purposely created each point in this book in a rhyming style so it will be easy to remember them. Let us take a moment to go over each point in its rhyming format:

POINT 1: "What I perceive is what I'll receive, so I must take control over what I believe!"

POINT 2: "When the storm comes, I need a safety tower; so I reach out to my "Higher Power.""

POINT 3: "I can change my course, it's never too late! But first I must stop and meditate."

POINT 4: "If I hold on to shame and guilt, my spirit will always be low. So, I will learn from my past, acknowledge my mistakes, and then simply let them go!"

POINT 5: "When life seems hopeless, I must change my point of view. That's how I regroup and figure out what I can do!"

POINT 6: "I am my greatest asset, the temple that holds my wealth. So, I must make me a priority and always care for "self.""

POINT 7: "Life without a mission is empty, dull, and worthless! In order to find fulfillment, I must discover my purpose."

POINT 8: "If I choose to be selfish, I'll always suffer from lack. To open the doors of abundance, I must learn how to give back."

POINT 9: "Despite my opposition and what others say or believe, I've got a made-up mind, no turning back. I'm determined to succeed!"

POINT 10: "My focus is my focus and my focus doesn't change. It's nothing you can do to make my focus rearrange!"

POINT 11: "If I purposely rid myself of all anger, worry, and strife, I'll learn to embrace each day, enjoying this journey of life!"

POINT 12: "Now that I have a plan, I know I won't fail! I'll practice every point, until I have them nailed!"

Now that you have all 12 points, it is up to you to memorize them. Make them into a song that you can quickly bring to your memory as you encounter a hardship. Write the points out on index cards and commit each one to memory. Place them on the refrigerator, the bathroom door, on your desk, or any other place where you are constantly able to review them. Become familiar with each point so you can figure out what to do, to counteract life's oppositions. As you review the points during hardships, you will quickly discover just what you can do at that moment to overcome your dilemma!

Internalize each point and continue to review and revise your Solution Book. Practice the techniques you learned and commit them to your everyday life.

Our journey together is coming to a close. You are now equipped with all the weapons you need to overcome any obstacle! The work you are willing to do on "self" will determine the results you will receive.

As you learn each point, share your discoveries with a friend. Practice the techniques in this book with them and share your progress. It is fun to work with someone you enjoy. They may also be able to share an experience with you to help you better internalize what you both have learned.

Congratulations! You have now finally completed this journey! You have all the tools you need to overcome. Push through, conquer and reclaim every dream! You were built to outlast the storm!!

July 1, 2017

It was a humid morning on June 1, 2017. I was up early filled with anticipation. For almost nine years, I envisioned the moment of when I would finally be released from prison after completing my sentence with good behavior, and the day was actually here. I pinched myself in disbelief, overwhelmed with joy that the day had finally arrived. I did what I thought I never had the strength to do. I survived close to a decade in prison!

Walking down the hills of West Virginia's Alderson Federal Prison Camp, all the valuable lessons I learned during my journey became so clear. I met many people who I may have never encountered in the free world, including Grammy Award-winning recording artist, Ms. Lauryn Hill. She and I remained close since her release from prison in 2014. From behind bars, we started a film production company, capturing several of the women who were released from prison, which we coordinated all through email. Now, it was finally my time for the camera crew to capture my own release.

With tears of joy streaming down my eyes, I hugged the many women I had bonded with, who helped me to complete my time. After my last goodbye, it was finally time to experience my fate.

When the prison doors swung open, the first faces I planted my eyes on was my parents and my children. I exited the prison and ran as quickly as I could into both of my children's loving arms. When I left, they were nine and eleven years old. Now they were eighteen and twenty-one years old. Although they were fully grown adults, I held them as if they were the babies I kissed on my sentencing day. The feeling I felt was like nothing I could ever imagine or think–VICTORY!!!

Exiting the prison in a luxury sprinter, the cameras turned on. For the first time on film, I began to share my story. I made a vow to God when He brought me through, I would tell the world of His goodness, grace and mercy. I knew it was important to share this experience to encourage someone else to push past the storm. Today, my greatest victory is knowing my pain was not in vain. My journey, both triumphs and failures, had purpose far greater than I could have ever hoped, dreamed or imagined. Life taught me by experience; I am indeed built to outlast the storm!

Made in the USA
Middletown, DE
29 August 2024

59653289R00113